Father Justin Taylor is an outstanding scholar. In recent years he has brought his prodigious scholarship to his research into the life and times of one French priest, Father Jean-Claude Colin (1790–1875). This resulted in a magnificent book, written in English, entitled "Jean-Claude Colin. Reluctant Founder". It is a long book, carefully crafted, beautifully written and invaluable in helping us understand the story and the context of the life of the Venerable Jean-Claude Colin and of the Religious Congregation that he founded. It is a pleasure to read.

Now Father Taylor has produced a new edition of this book which is considerably condensed. This version is to be published in several languages. We hope that this will make the inspiring life of the Venerable Jean-Claude Colin more widely known. Ideally, it will lead the reader to seek out the longer version of the story as well.

Father Taylor tells us the story of the post-Revolution French environment into which Father Jean-Claude was born and the response that he and his companions were to make in forming a Religious Congregation called the Society of Mary, or Marists.

The structures of the Catholic church had been torn apart by the French Revolution. Father Jean-Claude and his companions went into the remote mountains of the Bugey, in central France, and gave the people hope and encouragement by visiting them, listening to them and celebrating the Sacraments among them while preaching parish missions. The country was in constant political, economic and religious crisis. Father Jean-Claude and his companions responded by working to educate young people in secular and religious knowledge in schools and seminaries. The European world was opening its horizons by exploring a wider world. Jean-Claude and his companions organized missions into the furthest reaches of the Pacific, about as far from France as it was possible to go. All the while Father Jean-Claude and his companions were forming a family of Religious Congregations that thrived in his own time and continues to thrive today.

T0126323

The story of all that was achieved by Fr Jean-Claude Colin and his companions, both men and women, was guided by a simple, profound and accessible spirituality which looked to Mary as their guide on how to live and serve in their turbulent world. That spirituality continues to be the greatest gift that Marists offer the church and the world of our time. Father Justin Taylor's writings make this beautiful spirituality accessible to everyone.

We are grateful to Father Justin Taylor for offering us the opportunity to re-examine the story and offering us an insight into the extraordinary holiness and Gospel-based enthusiasm of Father Jean-Claude Colin. It is both a fascinating history for its own time and an inspiring story for our time.

John Larsen sm
Superior General of the Society of Mary
Feast of the Holy Name of Mary. September 12, 2021

A Short Life of Jean-Claude Colin, Marist Founder

Justin Taylor sm

Portrait of Jean-Claude Colin by Antoine Tollet (1857–1953) from photographs taken at the General Chapter of 1866.

A Short Life of Jean-Claude Colin, Marist Founder

Adapted from *Jean-Claude Colin, Reluctant Founder*

Justin Taylor sm

THEOLOGY
2021

Copy editor: Gabriel Bueno Siqueira
Cover design: Myf Cadwallader, Ron Nissen sm
Layout: Extel Solutions, India
Font: Minion Pro

ISBN: 978-1-922582-97-3   soft
           978-1-922582-98-0   hard
           978-1-922582-99-7   epub
           978-1-922737-00-7   pdf

Published and edited by

THEOLOGY

Making a lasting impact

An imprint of the ATF Press Publishing Group
owned by ATF (Australia) Ltd.
PO Box 234
Brompton, SA 5007
Australia
ABN 90 116 359 963
www.atfpress.com

Table of Contents

Photo Credits

Introductory Note

This short life of Jean-Claude Colin is abridged and adapted from the author's full biography, *Jean-Claude Colin, Reluctant Founder* (Hindmarsh, SA: ATF Press, 2018). It has been produced with the gracious permission of the publisher of that work, ATF Press Publishing Group. Readers who wish to have more information about the life of Jean-Claude Colin or about the sources used should consult the full biography.

My thanks are due to Alois Greiler sm, and to Ron Nissen sm, who read an earlier draft of this text and made very useful comments and suggestions for improving it. Many thanks also to those at ATF Press, Hilary D Regan and Gabriel B Siqueira, who worked on this project.

Chapter 1
Introducing Jean-Claude Colin

Jean-Claude Colin and the Society of Mary, of which he is a founding figure, belong in the large context of the response of French Catholicism—and more widely of European Christianity—to the challenge presented by the modern age. In France, the modern world burst on the scene in the great Revolution of 1789, which led to persecution of the Church. But, even without the drama and trauma of the Revolution, French Catholicism would have been severely challenged by the new civilisation that we identify as modernity. For the new ways of thinking that are conveniently called the Enlightenment, religious indifference, the rise of the middle classes to economic and political power, capitalism, industrialisation and urbanisation, the European discoveries of new lands and populations in the South Seas, all these new phenomena demanded a response on

the part of European Christianity. That response was by no means only negative. For the new age presented also new possibilities and aroused new vitality.

Colin was born a little over a year after the fall of the Bastille, on 7 August 1790. Before his fifth birthday, he had lost both his parents, victims, even martyrs, he believed of the Revolution through hardships suffered as a result of their support for their non-juring parish priest. He had childhood memories of

Memorial cross on the site of the Colin home on the slope of Crest, Le Barbery, Rhône, France.

clandestine Masses and priests on the run. These were experiences calculated to give him and not a few of his contemporaries an apocalyptic view of world history, which was at odds with the prevailing confidence in 'Progress'.

Not the least interesting thing about him was that he devised a new, and, it seems, unique response to the challenge of what we now call 'secularisation'. This he encapsulated in the expression: 'Unknown and hidden in this world.' In answer to what he regarded as the pride of the new age—in other words, its characteristic sense of human autonomy—he recommended humility and self-effacement, not only individual, but also corporate and institutional. In this he was inspired by his reading of the presence of Mary in 'the Church-as-it-was-coming-to-birth' [*l'Église naissante*]. His insight is as timely and needed now as it ever was.

He belongs to a remarkable generation of men and women who represent the response of French Catholicism to the new age with a vigorous and varied flowering of Catholic life, spirituality and apostolic action. One of the most important sectors of the Catholic revival was the region of Rhône-Alpes, centring on Lyons, at that time the second city of France and primatial see of 'the Gauls'. This region in fact formed a certain cultural, as well as geographical unity: the mother-tongue spoken by the rural populations of this region was not French, but the local *patois* or dialect of the language identified in modern times as Franco-Provençal, since it was related to but distinct from both the French spoken further north and the Provençal spoken further south. This language, which extended beyond France into Switzerland and even parts of Italy, never acquired a standard form that could be used as a written language, and, ever since the sixteenth century, French had been making its way in the region as the language of administration and formal instruction.

Lyons looks back to its martyrs of the second century, including its earliest bishops, Pothinus and Irenaeus, the servant-girl Blandina, and to many other saints through the ages, until modern times. Among the holy men and women of the post-Revolutionary diocese of Lyons are: Antoine Chevrier, founder of *l'Œuvre du Prado*; Pauline Jaricot, foundress of the Work of the Propagation of the Faith; Louis Querbes, founder of the Catechists of Saint Viator; Frédéric Ozanam (Lyonnais by adoption), founder of the Work of Saint Vincent de Paul; Jean-Pierre Néel, missionary priest, martyr.

On the eastern edge of the region, bordering on Switzerland and Savoy (once an independent duchy) lies the department of Ain, with its historic capital (but no longer administrative centre) and episcopal see at Belley. The pre-revolutionary diocese of Belley had also been home to many saints. The diocese restored in 1822 soon had a new roll of saints by birth or adoption, in first place, of course, the Curé of Ars, Jean-Marie Vianney; but also Jean-Baptiste Bottex, one of the victims of the massacre at Les Carmes on 3 September 1792; Gabriel Taborin (b. Belleydoux), founder of the Congregation of Brothers of the Holy Family of Belley; Rosalie Rendu, Sister of Charity.

Originally from Saint-Bonnet-de-Troncy (Rhône), Colin, as we shall see, spent a great part of his life in the department of Ain. Though not at all sure at first of his vocation to the priesthood, he studied at Saint-Jodard (Loire) and other minor seminaries, then at the Major Seminary of Saint-Irénée in Lyons. At this time, the diocese of Lyons, headed by Cardinal Fesch, uncle of the Emperor Napoleon, comprised the three departments of Loire, Rhône and Ain. This fact brought together as fellow-students young men whose paths may not otherwise have crossed. One year ahead of Colin was Jean-Marie Vianney, whom Colin consulted at Ars more than once in later life. Another fellow-seminarian, who was to become a close associate of Colin, was the future Saint Marcellin-Joseph-Benoît Champagnat, who was born at Marlhes, near Saint-Étienne (Loire) in 1789.

Chapter 2
The Society of Mary

Before their ordination on 22 July 1816, both Colin and Champagnat with several others had been recruited to a group aspiring to found a Society of Mary and who were to be called Marists. The initiator of this project was fellow-seminarian Jean-Claude Courveille, who had come to Saint-Irénée from Le Puy-en-Velay (Haute-Loire), where, kneeling in prayer before the Black Madonna in the Cathedral, he had 'heard' the Blessed Virgin say that she wanted a society called by her name to do her work. It was to be a kind of counterpart to the Society of Jesus, raised up, like Saint Ignatius' Company at the time of the Reformation, at a moment of crisis in the Church. They envisaged a life of preaching, catechising, hearing confessions in the rural and often abandoned parishes of the region, eventually, in a wider scope, education, even foreign missions.

The name Society of Mary was in the air at the end of the eighteenth and the beginning of the nineteenth centuries. Already, in 1792, during the period when the Society of Jesus was suppressed, Bernard Dariès gave it to a new project, which circulated among French exiles in Spain. In the same period, some former Jesuits regrouped under the name Society of Mary. It seems, however, that Courveille and his companions did not know of any of these ventures. In 1817, in Bordeaux, Guillaume-Joseph Chaminade, who knew nothing of what was afoot in Lyons, also founded a Society of Mary (Marianists). The name Marists, which Courveille believed also came from the Blessed Virgin herself, was not, in fact, used by any others.

For Jean-Claude Colin, the call of Mary was irresistible from infancy, when his dying mother had commended all her children, soon to be orphans, to the motherly care of the Blessed Virgin. Furthermore,

The ancient chapel of the Blessed Virgin, Fourvière, Lyons, where the Marist aspirants pledged to form the Society of Mary, July 23, 1816.

already before coming to the Major Seminary, he had been giving thought to some kind of apostolic institute under the name of Mary. Marcellin Champagnat, for his part, already had a plan for a congregation of teaching brothers and persuaded the other Marist aspirants to include them in the Society of Mary, which was also to comprise religious women and lay tertiaries. Let us note the relatively humble origin of all these young men, born into families of small rural proprietors or artisans. It may be an unexpected effect of the Revolution and its *égalité* that they felt competent to found a new religious society instead of looking to one of their social 'betters', typically a member of the minor nobility, as most religious founders had been until then. On 23 July 1816 the group, twelve in number, met for the last time at the Marian shrine of Fourvière, overlooking the city, where their leader Jean-Claude Courveille celebrated his first Mass and gave Holy Communion to his comrades; under the corporal during the celebration, they placed a document, which they had all signed, in which they pledged themselves to do all in their power to bring the Society of Mary into existence.

The newly ordained Jean-Claude Colin served his apprenticeship in priestly ministry as curate to his brother Pierre at Cerdon (Ain). Situated at the intersection of three valleys at the northern end of the Bugey Mountains, nineteen km. from Nantua, Cerdon was a staging post on the road from Lyons to Geneva; in 1832 it had a population of 1745. Vines grow on one of the nearby slopes, and Cerdon was and is still known regionally for its pleasant, lightly sparkling wine.

Cerdon had not escaped the effects of the extraordinary events of 1814–1816. The village, like the rest of the Bugey region and

The village of Cerdon in the northern Bugey region where the newly ordained
Jean-Claude Colin spent the first nine years of his priesthood, 1816–1825.

Lyons, was Bonapartist in sympathy. Cerdon had experienced the consequences of Napoleon's defeats in 1814 and 1815: invasion, by an Austrian army operating out of Switzerland, and war reparations. The region also suffered from the disastrous summer of 1816, and, by the winter months of 1817, many inhabitants were suffering real distress. These events, which were chronicled by the village schoolmaster, would certainly have had an impact on the newly arrived priests. We learn from the municipal records that Pierre Colin, as parish priest, was on a relief committee organised by the mayor, which decided to divert money destined for the repair of the church tower into an emergency fund.

The church, on a hill in the centre of the village, had been pillaged on 3 December 1793, its tower destroyed and its furniture burnt. After the restoration of regular worship with the concordat of 1801, Cerdon was served by a succession of priests. The parish that the Colin brothers came to was, by all indications, in a good state.

Jean-Claude soon recruited Pierre to the Marist project and began to write a rule for the Society of Mary. In 1817, Marcellin Champagnat, a curate at La Valla (Loire), began recruiting and training the first 'Little Brothers of Mary', and Pierre Colin invited two young women whom he knew, Jeanne-Marie Chavoin, born at Coutouvre (Loire) in 1786, and Marie Jotillon to come to Cerdon and begin the branch of Marist Sisters. In 1819, Jean-Claude made a vow to go to Rome, to reveal to the Holy Father what he believed to

Jeanne-Marie Chavoin, Foundress of the Marist Sisters.

be the supernatural origins of the Society.

The aspiring Marists did not, however, meet with favour for their project from the vicars general, who were governing the diocese of Lyons in the name of Cardinal Fesch, exiled in Rome after the downfall of his nephew Napoleon. They wanted to keep them exclusively in the service of the diocese, even to merge them with the newly founded diocesan missionaries of the Cross of Jesus

('Chartreux'). Discouraged, most of the original aspirants concluded that the project was going nowhere and drifted away. In these difficult times, Jeanne-Marie Chavoin encouraged and supported Pierre and Jean-Claude.

In January 1822, Courveille and the two Colin brothers wrote about their project to Pope Pius VII, who replied with cautious encouragement and directed them to see his nuncio in Paris. It was Jean-Claude Colin who made two journeys to the capital, where he showed his rule to the nuncio, Mgr Macchi, and also to the Sulpician Fathers, who remarked that it was more suited 'to angels than to men'.

It is likely that, if the Marists had submitted a simple plan for a congregation of priests engaged in mission preaching and education, and prepared to take on foreign missions, they would soon have gained approval from Rome. On the other hand, the plan for a multi-branch Society, comprising priests, religious sisters and brothers, and lay people, was to prove unacceptable. Furthermore, Colin's rule—of which only fragments are now extant—was not at all the kind of document that canonists required in a new religious group. For it was utopian, both in the sense of being highly idealistic, but also in the sense of being based on a vision of the Society of Mary's place in the Church and indeed in world history, which it is important to be acquainted with if we are to grasp the full truth of Jean-Claude Colin.

This utopian vision is expressed in the summary of the rules of the Society of Mary, which Colin composed in 1833: 'The general aim of the Society is to contribute in the best possible way, . . . to gather all the members of Christ, . . . so that at the end of time as at the beginning, all the faithful may with God's help be *one heart and one soul* [*cf* Acts 4:23] in the bosom of the Roman Church, and that all, walking worthily before God and under Mary's guidance, may attain eternal life.' Colin often repeated a saying that he attributed to Mary herself: 'I was the support of the Church at its birth; I will be so at the end of days.' He often said that the earliest Church—literally 'the-Church-as-it-was-coming-to-birth'—was the sole model for the Society of Mary. As he read the Acts of the Apostles, the ideal state of the Church had once been found in its earliest days, when Mary had been its support and all the believers were one in mind and heart and shared their possessions. He expected that it would come about at 'the end of time', when Mary would once again be the support of the Church. He believed that in this eschatological fulfilment, the Blessed Virgin had a key role, which she wanted her Society to carry out in her name. That was the purpose of its foundation and existence. In the meantime, the Society was to strive to bring about, and even to model, the 'new Church' that would resemble the Church of Acts. Such a perception of the role of a new congregation seeking approval could only appear unrealistic—perhaps even subversive—to hard headed Church authorities; indeed, it was to prove beyond the comprehension of many who were to join the Society of Mary.

In 1822 the diocese of Belley, comprising the department of Ain, was re-established. This meant that the would-be Marists now found themselves in two different dioceses and faced with two diocesan administrations. The nuncio sent the Marist file to the new Bishop of Belley.

Alexandre-Raymond Devie, born in 1767 at Montélimar (Drôme), was a remarkable man and a great bishop, who might have graced the episcopal sees of more prominent dioceses but chose to remain all his life at Belley. From the beginning, he devoted himself to the spiritual welfare of his flock, the organisation of the new diocese and the formation of clergy. He travelled tirelessly around the department of Ain in a carriage, which he had fitted up so that he could continue reading and writing on the road. He saw how the Marist priests and religious might play a part in the plans he had for his diocese, but had no intention of furthering their aim to gain papal approbation as a congregation at the service of the universal church.

In 1824, Bishop Devie gave a religious habit to Jeanne-Marie Chavoin and the young women who had joined her in community at Cerdon. He also permitted one of the few remaining Marist aspirants, Étienne Déclas, to join Pierre and Jean-Claude Colin at Cerdon, so that they could begin missions in neighbouring parishes. Meanwhile, near Saint-Chamond (Loire), Marcellin Champagnat and his brothers had constructed a large building, called 'the Hermitage', to serve as a mother house and centre of training for the Little Brothers of Mary, who were rapidly growing in numbers and establishing schools in many parishes. The multi-branch Society of Mary was thus moving from dream to reality.

Chapter 3
Mission Preacher in the Bugey

In 1825, Bishop Devie brought both communities of sisters and priests to Belley. The population of the episcopal city in 1832, six years after the arrival of the Marists, was given as 4286. Grass grew in its streets. Although Belley was about the same distance from Cerdon as Lyons, the Colin brothers and Jeanne-Marie Chavoin had never been there until they found themselves in the new diocese. Colin later marvelled that such a small, remote place should have been the birthplace of a Society that had acquired a global outreach; he could only compare it to Nazareth, the unlikely place where the Church began with the Holy Family.

Bishop Devie's pastoral plan for his diocese included systematic programmes of parish missions to strengthen and, where necessary, revive Catholic faith and practice after the turmoil initiated by the Revolution, and the consequent dislocation of the Church and the spread of religious indifference and alienation. In this context, Marist priests, who desired nothing more than to preach, catechise and hear confessions, could form a group of diocesan missionaries. Pope Leo XII proclaimed the year 1825 (extended into 1826) a year of Jubilee, the first since 1775, and, in his encyclical *Charitate Christi*, declared that he wished it to be a celebration of divine mercy, with as many as possible brought to the Sacrament of Penance, to obtain reconciliation and absolution.

This was music to the ears of Raymond Devie, who determined to use the Jubilee to counter the traditional rigorism of the French clergy in moral teaching and the administration of the Sacrament of Penance. Already, as Vicar General of the Diocese of Valence (Drôme), he had introduced the moral theology and confessional practice of Alphonsus Liguori, which were characterised by pastoral realism and a prudent middle way between excessive rigour and laxity. His beatification in 1816 had given the stamp of papal approval to his teaching and promoted it outside his native Italy. Devie followed up the papal encyclical of 1825 with his own circular letter of 26 September 1826 to all the priests of his diocese. The Jubilee was to be the moment for redoubling zeal and efforts to reach out to those who were alienated from the Church by laxity or indifference, rather than by 'impiety'. It would be celebrated in the diocese for six months from November 1826, during which the faithful would be able to fulfil the conditions for gaining the Jubilee plenary indulgence by confession, communion, visits to designated churches and prescribed prayers, and thus obtain full remission of the remaining debt of 'temporal—as opposed to eternal—punishment' still due to forgiven sin. Where possible, bands of mission preachers would go round the parishes of the dioceses; where that was not possible, the local clergy would organise a 'retreat' of several weeks.

The bishop set out the subjects that should be covered in the mission or retreat sermons, including the Apostles' Creed, the commandments of the God and the Church, the sacraments, prayer. He himself would try to come each time, to confer Confirmation and take part in the exercises. As for the confessional, he referred his priests to the encyclical *Charitate Christi* and specifically to the pope's direction that confessors should show 'much goodness and charity towards sinners'. Besides reading the encyclical, priests should also study Alphonsus' work *Praxis confessariorum*, copies of which would be available at the seminary at Brou and at the diocesan office in Belley.

As curate at Cerdon, Jean-Claude Colin had had occasion to feel uncomfortable with the rigorist moral code that he had imbibed at Saint-Irénée but lacked the confidence to question it. Under the guidance of the bishop and Bl Alphonsus he began a gradual development towards fully embracing Liguorian doctrine and practice for himself and for the Society of Mary.

The band of Marist mission preachers slowly grew in numbers, as already ordained priests were attracted to their ministry and to their Marian spirituality. The mission territory assigned to them by the bishop was the Bugey, the mountainous region lying between Cerdon and Belley. Most places they visited were little, often remote, rural villages, with populations of a few hundred. An exception was Tenay, a small industrial town specialising in weaving, whose population (1130 in 1832) included industrial workers and middle-class mill owners. They also gave retreats at the seminaries of Belley and Meximieux.

The village of Lacoux in the Bugey mountains visited by Jean-Claude Colin and the pioneer missioners in the winter of 1825.

The missions could take place only during the winters, when farming folk were freer to attend church frequently. The terrain could be arduous, and the climate harsh. Living conditions were usually of the simplest, and the missionaries frequently had to 'rough it'. What they found from parish to parish could also differ enormously, from well kept churches and presbyteries, to dirt and neglect, and from communities practising their faith with dedicated pastors, to indifference and hostility, where the priest (if there was one) was often a major part of the problem.

The Marists met the different situations with simplicity and detachment from self-interest. They avoided occasioning unnecessary expense, cheerfully accepting whatever was provided by way of accommodation or food, making do with the furnishings or equipment they found in the church (no need for a confessional or a pulpit—they could be improvised, two candles would suffice instead of six, copes were not indispensable . . .). Above all, they avoided causing offence or embarrassment to the pastor or taking his place at table or in church.

The missions followed a standard pattern, which could be adapted or developed. They began with the children—a practice recommended by Jean-Marie Vianney—teaching them their catechism and telling them about the mission and asking them to pray for their parents. They heard the confessions of children of an age to receive Holy Communion; the grown-ups soon followed. Catechetical instruction continued throughout the mission, and the church was always full of adults as well as children.

We are well informed about the structure of the mission, the subjects of instruction and the various ceremonies that took place within it. The plan reveals a strategy of convincing and converting that appears to have been successful. The spoken word was illustrated and reinforced by paraliturgical ceremonies that could be dramatic. Prayer was at the basis of the mission, as the missionaries prayed daily and got others to pray for the conversion of sinners. On arrival at the parish—always quietly and unobtrusively—they knelt and prayed for the souls in purgatory who belonged to the place, then rose and recited the *Memorare*, commending the mission to Our Lady. Each instruction began with three 'Hail Marys'. The opening instruction was an invitation to take part in the mission, followed by a sermon on the mercy of God. The address that Colin wrote for this occasion still exists. In it he describes the missionaries as 'the instruments of God's mercies for you'—indeed 'most unworthy instruments'. He emphasised that they too were human, subject to the same weakness as his hearers and therefore knowing 'how far human frailty can go'. So the people should have no fear or mistrust in revealing their own sins in confession.

The topics of the first week, beginning with the Apostles' Creed, were designed to win the confidence of the hearers, although from Day Four the preachers began to shake them up a little. Then followed the explanations of the Ten Commandments. Here too care was taken not to discourage the hearers: the preachers did not at first go into much detail about the obligations of the commandments, but encouraged the people to come to confession, thus showing good will and a beginning of conversion. It seems to have been regular

Pulpit of the church of St Mary Magdalene, Prémilieu, where in the summer of 1827 the Marists preached the only mission not conducted during the winter.

practice not to give absolution at this first confession, but to instruct penitents and tell them to return later in the mission and continue their confession. After most people had approached the sacrament of penance this first time, the missionaries began to tell their hearers more exactly what the commandments required and to embark on such subjects as the malice of sin and the punishment it deserved. At this point in the mission, there was a Requiem Mass for all the dead of the parish, with sermons on death and purgatory, followed by a procession to the cemetery carrying the pall that usually covered the coffin, with a final sermon on death at the cemetery cross.

About midway in the mission, there was a sermon on the confidence one should have in the Blessed Virgin, followed by a procession with the statue of Our Lady during which litanies and hymns were sung in her honour. The following day a particularly impressive and moving ceremony was held. All the children came to Mass with their parents, and the preacher asked them if they wanted to choose the Blessed Virgin as their mother

The church of St Laurence, Innimont, site of the Marist mission of Nov 1826.

and protector, to which no doubt they all replied, 'Yes'. The preacher continued that Mary wanted children who were good and obedient, so they should ask pardon of their parents for all the times they had been disobedient. He then bade the parents withdraw all the curses they had pronounced against their children. By this time, many were in tears. Finally parents and clergy present held out their hands over the children and consecrated them to the Blessed Virgin.

Other subjects of instruction were the Sacraments, especially Baptism, Penance and the Eucharist. By now most parishioners would have returned to the confessional, continued their confessions in the light of their deeper understanding of human sin and divine grace, and received absolution. A further impetus to conversion was given by a striking ceremony, for which the Blessed Sacrament was exposed on a specially constructed altar in the middle of the church. There was a sermon on mortal sin; then all the priests present took off their surplices, prostrated themselves before the Blessed Sacrament and asked God's forgiveness.

The next big occasion centred on Baptism and the accompanying promises and obligations that had been given and undertaken by godparents on behalf of each child baptised shortly after birth. The people were asked to give their assent to each article of the Creed by saying 'I believe' and raising the lighted candles they held. Next followed the promise to observe each of the commandments. By now the parish would be deemed ready for the general Communion that would be announced. The final act of the mission was, by custom, the blessing of a commemorative cross, such as can still be seen in many places in France. Because of the expense involved, however, the Marists' practice was not to propose a 'cross-planting', but to have it only if the parish spontaneously asked for it.

Impressive as such ceremonies were, at the heart of the mission were the long hours spent in the pulpit and the confessional, instructing and moving the hearts of the people and encouraging them to conversion and repentance. Let us not forget also the many hours the missionaries spent every day in prayer, with their breviary and in personal meditation. The key to it all was mercy. Reminiscing some years later, Colin reflected on the ministry of the preacher: 'We must be kind. And after all, what is the difference between them and us? They are our brothers. The whole difference between them and us is that we are the ones doing the talking, and these poor folk can't answer back.'

There was another context in which these Marist missions and similar preaching campaigns were conducted. After the defeat of the Emperor Napoleon, the old monarchy was restored, in the person of the late king's brother, Louis XVIII. There were those in the church, as in wider society, who saw this as an opportunity to restore as much as possible of the *ancien régime*, and it was not unknown for revival missions to include triumphalist demonstrations of the return to power of a church arm-in-arm with the state ('the alliance of throne and altar'). Colin and his companions were personally pleased with the restoration of the Bourbons; wisely, however, they avoided any such manifestations or propaganda. It was a policy continued through the succeeding years, expressed in statements by Colin such as: 'Remember, Messieurs, that we are not for changing the government but for saving souls.' The Society was not to be identified with any political opinion: 'In adopting one shade of opinion we necessarily alienate all those of a different political colour, while we are for saving everyone.'

During the summer months and between missions, the small band of Marist missionaries lived at the Minor Seminary in Belley and worked on their sermons and instructions. Their living conditions were far from ideal. They were lodged in the attic, in rooms that were improvised and cramped, and they suffered from the heat of the summer and the cold of the winter. They took their meals with the professors of the Seminary, some of whom openly mocked the Marists as 'Volume Two of the Society of Jesus, bound in asses' hide'; their example spread to the students. They did, however, win the respect of the superior, Monsieur Pichat, who even expressed his desire to join them. They also received the practical help and support of the Marist Sisters, who were installed nearby at Bon-Repos. Jean-Claude Colin took a full part in the missions from 1826 to 1829. In March 1826, Bishop Devie designated him superior of the Marist mission preachers of the diocese.

In the middle of 1826 the nascent Society of Mary fell into a deep crisis. We have been following the career of Jean-Claude Colin and his companions at Belley. In the Diocese of Lyons Jean-Claude Courveille had been busy establishing communities of teaching brothers and sisters, whose relationship to those of Marcellin Champagnat and Jeanne-Marie Chavoin is not clear. He also regarded himself as superior general of the entire Society of Mary, a claim that was accepted by some, including Marcellin Champagnat, but not by all. Relations between the two Jean-Claudes were never, it seems, warm, and both Colin brothers occasionally acted independently of Courveille, while acknowledging his *de facto* leadership.

In May 1826 Courveille committed an unspecified sexual act with a brother postulant—almost certainly a minor—at the Hermitage and withdrew for a 'retreat' at the Trappist abbey of Aiguebelle (Drôme). The fact became known to Étienne Terraillon, one of the remaining signatories of the act of commitment of 1816, who was also living at the Hermitage, and who informed the diocesan authorities. Champagnat, in the mean time, had received a letter from Courveille at Aiguebelle speaking at length of his unworthiness to be a Marist, in terms that could be read as a resignation from the group. Terraillon recommended Champagnat, and also Colin, who arrived unexpectedly at the Hermitage as the crisis broke, to accept Courveille's resignation with immediate effect. When they hesitated, as they were still in the dark about what had happened, Terraillon must have told them enough of what he knew to decide them to follow his advice. From that moment, Courveille was excluded from the nascent Society and prevented from re-entering when he asked to do so some years later.

That left the little Society of Mary with the disturbing question, How could the original message be genuinely from Mary, if the recipient of that message and founder and leader of the group turned out to be so unworthy? The Marists continued to believe that Mary had indeed 'spoken', while at the same time doing their best to expunge Courveille from their collective memory. They were also now without any acknowledged over-all leader and remained so for several years.

In March 1829 Jean-Claude Colin conducted his final mission at Ruffieu, in the Valromey. The bishop himself came towards the end of the month and confirmed 600 children, many of them from neighbouring parishes. The church was small, and another preacher, stationed in the tribune, relayed Colin's sermon to the crowds outside through a window. The bishop brought with him the news that the Superior of the Minor Seminary, M. Pichat, had died. He instructed Colin to return immediately to Belley, to help his brother Pierre prepare the students for Easter. In fact, he had decided that Jean-Claude's days on the road were over. On the evening of Easter Sunday (9 April) Devie sent for Colin and told him to take charge of the Seminary the following day. The appointment came as an unwelcome shock, and Colin asked for three days to make a retreat and pray that the bishop would change his mind. Devie simply told him to take charge immediately.

In the life of many persons there is a period to which they look back as 'the heroic age', a time when they struggled with difficulties, but which they think of nevertheless as 'the best'. For Jean-Claude Colin the period to which he frequently looked back as 'the good time', despite its hardships, were those years, from January 1825 to March 1829, during which he preached missions in the Bugey mountains.

Chapter 4
School Principal

The establishment that Colin was taking over had been founded in 1751 as a college run by religious priests. It reopened after the revolution, in 1803, under the direction of the 'Fathers of the Faith' (former Jesuits and their more recent emulators). It was during this period that the writer, poet and statesman Alphonse de Lamartine, after whom the school is now named, was a student. In 1808, it came under the control of the municipality but eventually went into decline. It was due to close in 1823, when Bishop Devie obtained authorisation to bring it under diocesan control as a minor seminary. The school continued, however, to keep a mixed character, educating boys who were not in any way destined for the priesthood alongside seminarians.

The college of Belley where the first Marists came to live in 1825 and where Jean-Claude Colin was appointed principal in 1829.

Colin's appointment fell at a sensitive period in church-state relations in France. At the beginning of 1828, the conservative government had felt the need to make concessions to liberal opinion and chose to do so in the field of education, where there was much opposition to ecclesiastical control. Some of the measures taken affected the Belley establishment. On 16 June King Charles X, after much heart-searching, signed two decrees (*ordonnances*) that put the minor seminaries under closer government control. The first subjected eight seminaries hitherto run by the Jesuits to the 'University', that is, the public education system; it also required all superiors and teachers at minor seminaries to declare that they did not belong to any religious congregation not legally established in France. The second decree regulated the number of seminaries and their students and the scholarships that funded them; it also required government recognition of the appointment of superiors. Bishop Devie, like the other bishops, had protested against what they regarded as infringements of their rights; but, when mollifying explanations came from the government, he decided to follow the new regulations. On 24 April 1829, Devie wrote to the minister for ecclesiastical affairs, seeking approval for the appointment of Jean-Claude Colin in succession to Monsieur Pichat, deceased; this was granted on 3 May. Since the Marists were not yet a congregation, Colin's appointment strictly conformed to the government requirement. He was thirty-eight years old, already middle-aged, as these things were reckoned in those days, but in his prime.

We get an idea of the school that Colin took over from the replies sent in by Bishop Devie on 27 February 1828 to a questionnaire from the ministry for ecclesiastical affairs. There were 200 students, of whom twenty paid no boarding fees, most of the others paid between ten and twenty francs a month, and some few paid between thirty and fifty francs. The establishment had no revenues and, in addition to fees paid by the students, its only resources were the 'sacrifices' made by the bishop and clergy of the diocese. There were thirty dayboys, essentially choristers and altar servers from the cathedral. The subjects taught covered the entire curriculum from elementary classes teaching children to read and write through to the highest college level, with classes in French, Greek, Latin, rhetoric, philosophy and mathematics. Plainchant was also taught; but not music, dancing or fencing. Some students had obtained the baccalaureate of the university. In 1827, forty-three graduates had passed on to the major seminary at Brou. The students usually wore ordinary clothes, but for Sundays and Feast Days there was a uniform consisting of a dark coloured overcoat for the younger boys and a soutane for those seniors who were going on for theology. The youthful staff, who numbered twelve, consisted of diocesan priests or clerics destined for priestly ministry in the diocese.

The fact that the college was also a minor seminary meant that the cathedral clergy felt free to require the students to take part in the liturgy there on certain feast days and to call on the priests of the college staff to conduct services from time to time. Colin succeeded in reducing the attendance of the students to taking part in the annual Corpus Christi procession. He also put a stop to 'borrowing' his teachers for the cathedral on class days, retorting: 'When you send me professors to teach class, I will send you canons to take services.' The cathedral dignitaries complained to the bishop; but he stood by his headmaster.

Jean-Claude accepted his appointment on condition that the college would be entrusted to the Marists. He had in any case soon realised that his appointment to the college, along with his brother as spiritual director, had a significance wider than simply a post to be filled or a task to be performed on behalf of the bishop. At least as early as the letter to Pope Pius VII, the Marists had declared that one of the goals of the Society of Mary was 'to train youth in every way to knowledge and virtue'. Now was the chance for the priests, as well as the brothers, to turn that aspiration into reality. Gradually, as they grew in number, Marists were appointed to the Belley school.

Over several years Colin had been able to observe the school closely and realised that there were tensions both among the students and also among his staff. He needed to establish his authority quickly in the house. The student body was made up of at least three quite distinct groups. Most students were seminarians who had begun and were continuing their studies in Belley. There was also a second student bloc, consisting of philosophy students who had hitherto received their formation at the other minor seminary at Meximieux. Although they too were preparing for ministry in the same diocese, they apparently displayed a 'marked repugnance' for having to spend one or two years with their colleagues at Belley and did not form a homogeneous community with them. Then there were the lay students, survivors of the old municipal college, who had kept their 'college boy' spirit and passed it on to the seminarians. Colin recalled that, although the students' behaviour during the rest of the school year after he took over was 'fairly good', he expelled six or seven, and told the others to make up their mind where they stood. When the new school year began, at All Saints 1829, about forty did not return. On the other hand, the intake was numerous, and the year that followed was noted for 'piety and good behaviour'.

His colleagues, he later said, gave him even more trouble than their pupils. In fact, one of the greatest trials that befell the Society was having to live with 'colleagues who thought we were mad, who did not enter into our way of thinking, who acted against us'. In the first month, 'every teacher' was coming to him with advice: 'You have to do this, you have to change that'. Finally, he spoke his mind at a council meeting: he had no intention of departing in any respect from the ways of his predecessor and did not want to hear any more talk of changes. At the end of the year Colin told one teacher not to return. During the summer vacation, in fact, a number of other staff changes were made.

When the staff reassembled after the summer vacation at All Saints 1829, the new principal laid before them a brief treatise (fifteen pages) on education he had composed, which combined general principles with comments tailored to the situation of the school. In doing this Colin was showing a remarkable self-assurance. He had taken over as principal without any experience of teaching—a fact of which senior members of his staff were well aware and prepared to remind him. Besides his own observations and ideas of best practice, he was also adept at consulting and reading what were regarded as the best authors. In this case, he had spent part of the summer reading a well-known educational work from the early eighteenth century. This was Charles Rollin's *Traité des études*, first published in Paris between 1726 and 1731, and considered throughout the eighteenth and well into the nineteenth centuries in France as a major educational authority. That book is not in fact a treatise on education as we might understand the term today; it is, on the whole, rather a manual for a teacher of humanities and rhetoric and deals with the content of the classical curriculum and the best way to teach it. Rollin begins and ends his book with pedagogical material on which Colin drew largely.

This short treatise is in fact the only substantial composition by Colin that is not a religious rule. It shows his powers of assimilation and synthesis. He was not an educational reformer. We should not look for originality in the content of his text. What he writes there could all be found elsewhere, whether in older authors or in his contemporaries, some of whom were innovators in a way he had no intention of being. On the other hand, his personal synthesis and appropriation of his source have some original features and indicate well his sharp perception of the educational environment.

A striking example of his perceptiveness is to be found immediately in the title he gave to his treatise: *Avis à messieurs les professeurs, préfets, directeurs* et supérieur *du petit séminaire de Belley* So he is addressing not only his staff—teachers, prefects, directors—but also the superior or principal (that is himself), thus from the outset expressing his solidarity with them. It is consistent with this approach that, throughout the work, the pronoun most often used is 'we'. He never writes 'you', telling the staff what they are to do: 'we' are all together in this enterprise. A glance at the plan of the document brings out the fact that Colin's instructions are essentially about relationships between persons and groups of persons. His opening words declare that to educate a person is already a 'sublime task', and to educate him in a Christian way is a 'heavenly work'. The principal duties of educators are to make of their pupils 'Christians, upright gentlemen (*hommes honnêtes et polis*), and lastly men of learning (*savants*)'.

Five qualities were required in the educator: authority; understanding the students; a good quality of instruction; example; vigilance. Authority was to be gained through respect rather than instilled by fear. Discipline, especially rewards and punishments, should take into account the mentality of the boy, including his sense of fairness. Among the range of punishments available, corporal punishment is not mentioned—which contrasts with the floggings customary in English schools at the time. Members of staff were to form a community, with a common life, sharing prayers and meals.

It is clear from all the above that Colin's instructions are not written specifically for the training of candidates for the priesthood but can fit any school. Three aspects of his educational thought may be seen as distinctive: a healthy cheerfulness; not too many religious observances; a plan for each individual. A school conducted according to the spirit of Colin's instructions would be a safe and friendly environment where boys and young men could grow up and learn religious, moral and human values as well as the standard curriculum.

Chapter 5
'Centre of Unity'

Since the eclipse of Courveille in 1826, the aspiring Marists—sisters, brothers and priests—lived and worked in the two dioceses of Belley and Lyons, without any common leader, recognised at least among themselves. The most likely outcome would have been the splitting of the Marists into two groups affiliated to their respective dioceses. That process was already happening, under pressure from reality and from the diocesan authorities, who wanted the Marists, but as their own instruments. The Marists, however, wanted to stay united. So, in the autumn of 1830—but not till four years after Courveille's departure—the priests of the two diocesan groups came together in Belley and elected Jean-Claude Colin as 'centre of unity' or, as he was also called, 'central superior'. This was not the recognition or formalising of any position that Colin already held. Since all the Marists priests in the Belley diocese lived at the college-seminary, he was in fact superior of all of them. But this was by appointment of the bishop, and, if there had been other communities of Marist priests in the diocese, he would not necessarily have been their superior. As for Lyons, of course, he had no position regarding the priests and brothers at the Hermitage, who were under Marcellin Champagnat.

Why, then, was Colin chosen? He had proved his commitment to the Society by already drafting a rule and vowing to go to Rome, by being a co-signatory, with his brother Pierre and Courveille, of the letter to Pope Pius VII, and by taking the rule to the nuncio in Paris. In fact, the field was not wide. Of the original signatories of the 1816 act of commitment, only four remained, and really only two would have been considered, namely Colin and Champagnat. Marcellin was fully occupied with the brothers, which left Colin as the only real candidate. To say this is not to depreciate Jean-Claude Colin, but to give relief and perspective to his achievement. Colin's greatness consisted in the fact that he stepped up and took responsibility for the future of a body that he had not initiated—while believing and insisting that he was no more than a provisional superior holding the fort until someone more suitable could take over.

At this point in his life, let us pause to ask, What was he like? First of all, his appearance. Jean-Claude Colin was short (1.64 meters or 5 foot 4 inches in height) and somewhat stout. He had an oval-shaped face and a wide, high forehead. His hair, which fell around his ears, must originally have been brown, to judge from his eyebrows, but turned prematurely white. His complexion was fair and his eyes bluish-grey. He had an aquiline nose and a determined chin.

This last named feature expressed a forceful character, which was somewhat belied by a manner that could easily make him seem, as one observer put it, like 'one of those good, little old country priests, very simple, very timid, not knowing where to put themselves to take up less space'. In addition, he was careless of his appearance. He followed the fashion of his youth in being clean-shaven, rather than growing a beard as many clerics did in the nineteenth century. Often, however, his chin exhibited several days' growth, and his soutane bore snuff stains. A speech impediment, which he largely overcame, left him with a permanent tendency to pronounce all sibilant consonants as 'sh'. Those who knew Colin, however, recognised the intellectual grasp and the personal ascendancy that made him a leader of men.

On the other hand, the impression of shyness and diffidence had once corresponded to his demeanour as a boy and a young man. Those who had known him then would have been very surprised to encounter in later life the man who, it was said, 'did things on a grand scale . . . . [and] walked not with measured step but with giant strides, which, granted, tended to splash mud on the next man'. At the same time, Colin, even when he was leader of the Marists, would frequently hesitate to take decisions that seemed to others to be obvious, while he waited for certainty that this was the will of God. Even admirers were forced to wonder whether he was 'perhaps too awkward in his business dealings', noting that he 'ran into difficulties with a great many of those who had dealings with him, both inside and outside [the Society]'. Periods of great energy would, characteristically, be followed by spells of inaction. Throughout his life, he yearned for solitude and made repeated attempts to lay down his office.

Colin's election as 'central superior' of the Marists had taken place against the background of the July Revolution, which toppled Charles X and brought Louis Philippe d'Orléans to the throne. By the beginning of the new school year in November 1830, continuing political and social unrest were beginning to have an enormous impact even upon the college-seminary at Belley. Looking back, Colin considered it his 'masterpiece' to have kept the school going through the year 1830–1831. He came through this trying time as a tested and acknowledged leader.

Julien Favre, who was to succeed Colin as superior general, was a student in rhetoric at the Belley college in 1830–1831 and recalled what it was like to live through those times. The students began with passive protests against authority and non-cooperation. If one was punished, everyone would be on his side. The word would go round, 'No singing at Vespers', and no one opened their mouth. If anyone dared to break the embargo, he was beaten up. To show their discontent, students paraded around the school building in silence save for the tramp of their feet on the pavement. Then the peasants came down from the mountains carrying rifles—real or imitation—as in 1790. This put the students into a real revolutionary fervour, which spread to the teachers. On one day off, for the customary recreational walk, the students removed their uniforms, carried wooden axes and marched like a battalion in formation singing the 'Marseillaise' and other revolutionary songs 'with a sort of frenzy as if drunk'. One of the teachers also took part in this demonstration. They arrived at a forest, where they began yelling and behaving in such a way that Pierre Colin, who was with them, was afraid they were going to kill him.

We do not have many details about how Colin handled the insurrection in the college. He had to face it largely alone. It appears that, through much of this time, Raymond Devie was out of action as he recovered from a cataract operation, which in those days involved immobilising the patient for a long time while the wound healed; there was danger of death, and full recovery was slow. Colin was thus without the bishop's active support when he needed it and seems to have found the interventions of the vicars general more of a hindrance than a help. As for his colleagues, with a few exceptions, notably his brother, he seems to have had little support and from some quarters open rebellion. Several signified their adherence to the new tendencies by subscribing publicly—and against the express disapproval of the bishop—to *L'avenir*, the liberal Catholic newspaper edited by the Comte de Montalembert, who called for the separation of Church and State.

There was a rumour of a plot among some of the staff to oust Colin, which would fit a moment when he was isolated and vulnerable. Those colleagues who were especially rebellious would have seen their chance to overthrow authority, while others could have imagined that, by sacrificing Colin, they might placate the students. Townspeople even expected to hear from day to day that he had been assassinated. Colin kept calm and remained in control. Favre was quite sure that, had it not been for him, the college-seminary would not have survived the crisis. The diocese of Belley owed much to him, and no doubt Bishop Devie realised that and was grateful. There was, however, a price to be paid in Colin's own health. His hair turned white, and he was prematurely aged. Colin himself spoke of the damage that constant anxiety and lack of sleep did to his health.

Having succeeded in bringing the college through the crisis, Colin had earned the right to have things the way he wanted: it was to be a Marist establishment. He wrote to the confreres at the Hermitage that he was thinking of giving it 'a new way of going about things (*marche*) that would fit in with our goal'. Beginning with the new school year, all teachers were to be affiliates of the Society, and there would be a vice-superior who would also be master of novices. We also hear of structural changes: the students were separated according to age into three divisions, each having its own study and dormitory and its own recreational outing; the masters had their own dining room. The school year that opened in November 1831 saw a number of further changes in the staff—those who had subscribed to *L'avenir* did not return.

One of the means by which the Marist priests of the two dioceses could develop a sense of unity was by joining in a common retreat. At the end of the retreat held in September 1831, all who took part—including members of staff of the Belley college—signed an act of consecration to Our Lady, which signified their affiliation to the Society of Mary. Among the new signatories was Pierre Chanel. A priest of the diocese of Belley since 1827, he had felt a vocation for the foreign missions and, along with colleagues Claude Bret and Denis Maîtrepierre, thought at one stage of applying to go to America, goal of many French missionaries. That he adhered to the Marists may have been due to an expectation that they were going to undertake foreign missions—a work, which they envisaged but which they had so far made no move to engage in. At the same time as he joined the Marist priests at the Belley college, his sister Françoise entered the convent of Marist sisters at Bon-Repos. Chanel was first assigned to teaching, then was appointed successively spiritual director (autumn 1832) and vice-superior (autumn 1834); the latter post meant effectively head of the day-to-day administration on behalf of Colin, who remained superior but now had many others concerns to occupy his time and attention.

La Capucinière, Belley, where the Marist community was established in 1832.

The chapel steps of La Capucinière, Belley, on which the pioneer Marists knelt during the first professions in 1836.

Up till now the Marist priests of Belley lacked a house of their own. For Colin the last months of 1832 were much occupied by the project to take over a former Capuchin friary in Belley known for that reason as 'La Capucinière'. Secularised in 1791, the property had been acquired in 1826 by Bishop Devie, who intended it to be the residence of the group of diocesan missionary priests he wanted to found on the model of the 'Chartreux' of Lyons. It was probably at the end of 1831 that the bishop proposed letting the Marists use the house. In November 1832 a community of three priests and several coadjutor brothers (at first called 'Joseph brothers') were able to move in. At last the Marists of Belley had their own house, where they could live the religious life and receive candidates for training. The priests engaged in the college-seminary continued to live there. Colin, who had not yet been permitted by Bishop Devie to transfer to La Capucinière, came and went between the two houses, which, he told Champagnat, 'made only one': he was, of course, superior of both.

The Capuchin friary formed a rectangle around an interior courtyard. One side was taken up by a public chapel or church, adjoined by a smaller chapel or choir, where the friars had recited the divine office. The church had not been a place of worship since the Revolution, and, before Bishop Devie acquired it, had been used as a theatre and a dance hall. Initially, the Marists had use only of the south side of the building and half of the courtyard, while a sitting tenant occupied the rest. In the following year, they had the whole house to themselves.

From the first, the Marist priests at La Capucinière continued to preach missions in the diocese. After 1834, the former Capuchin friary began to serve also as a house of formation. At this time, most candidates for the priests' branch of the Society were already ordained, and there was as yet no formal novitiate. So the training to be offered at La Capucinière was at first destined for only a very small number of students. After the approbation of the Society, in September 1836, which entailed permission to profess the vows of religion, a canonical novitiate was needed, also for those who were already priests before they joined.

Colin also decided to open a small boarding school at La Capucinière, which continued in existence until 1840. This was the first educational establishment that belonged to the Marist priests (as distinct from the college-seminary, which they staffed, but which belonged to the diocese). It began very modestly. In fact, there was no attempt to provide classes for them in the house, and they followed the courses at the college-seminary. Subsequently, the school took a small number of boarders from local well-to-do families and gave classes to the younger boys, while older pupils went to the college.

It was hardly a brilliant beginning, with either the house of formation or the boarding school. The establishment, or, perhaps better, experiment, was very fragile and did not at first inspire confidence. Confreres were discouraged and even alarmed. 'What if everyone left?', was the question that Claude Bret put one day to Jean-

Claude Colin, who replied instantly and forcefully: 'If everyone left, I would sing the *Te Deum* and I would start again.'

An incident concerning the Belley boarding school illustrates very well Colin's idea that the Marists were to be 'instruments of the divine mercies'. One of the boys was the son of General Louis Carrier, who lived in Belley, where he was well known not to practise his Catholic religion. When the general fell ill, Colin had hoped that Jean-Marie Millot, prefect of the establishment, would be able to reconcile him with the Church. The general, however, did not want the Viaticum (communion given to the dying) brought to him publicly, as was usual, but asked that it be brought privately after dark. Colin believed that the general had enough good will to warrant acceding to his request, and, when the vicar general disagreed, went to the bishop, who told him to do as M. Carrier requested. Before he died on 30 October 1838, the general had not only received the sacraments, but had openly blessed his son and asked the household servants to pray for him—'He did much more than was asked of him', was Colin's comment.

Jean-Claude's authority over the whole Society of Mary in this period was moral rather than legal. Nevertheless, he believed that he had been given—even if only provisionally—a responsibility and the authority to carry it out. At least in his own mind, he was more than a mere negotiator or go-between, able to advise and persuade, but not to command. On the other hand, both the limits of his authority and its manner of working were undefined and could only be clarified by trial and, occasionally, error. He might invoke obedience; but would others consider themselves bound to obey? The Marists had already had one bad experience with Courveille of a would-be 'superior general', who tried to exercise an authority that others did not think he had. They would be sensitive to any attempt by Colin to overstep the mark. Breadth and flexibility were going to be needed both by the central superior and by his confreres. There was plenty of room for misunderstandings. And they occurred.

Then, too, there was the question of Colin's position with regard to the diocesan authorities of Lyons. In their eyes, he was simply a priest of another diocese, with no standing to intervene in the Lyons diocese, even when it concerned the Marists there. In other words, they did not recognise him as any sort of religious superior. Colin's immediate concern was to keep the priests of the two dioceses together and with the same spirit and way of life. He was, of course, more intimately linked with the Belley priests, whose life and ministry he shared and whose superior he was. He was less well known to those of Lyons; yet now, for the sake of unity, he exercised oversight over them too. Not long after Colin's election as central superior, Marcellin Champagnat had been elected superior ('provincial') of the Lyons priests, a position that was ratified by the diocesan authorities of Lyons. The relationship between the two was going to be crucial. Fortunately, they knew each other well and respected each other highly; and they had a long-established habit of communication.

Champagnat was also, of course, the superior of the teaching brothers. Up till now, Colin had tended to regard the brothers as rather marginal to the Society of Mary and essentially Champagnat's concern; Marcellin, for his part, had always kept him informed about their affairs. From now on, Colin accepted that they were fully an integral part of the Society and had to give them greater attention, not simply out of fraternal interest but—in some sense not easy to define and, in particular, to coordinate with Champagnat's authority—as their ultimate superior. Then there were the Marist sisters, who, had been considered from the beginning as a branch of the Society of Mary: the central superior was responsible for them too; and yet they had their own superior, Mother Saint-Joseph (Jeanne-Marie Chavoin). All this made for a situation of considerable complexity.

All this time, Colin was working for the recognition of the Society of Mary as a supra-diocesan congregation. Devie, on the other hand, wanted the Marists of Belley to be entirely under his control. Over the years, the bishop tried everything to win Colin over. Jean-Claude, however, put up an unshakeable resistance, and felt that sometimes the bishop exerted unfair pressure. On one occasion, he realised that he was feeling a great antipathy towards Raymond Devie and decided to take heroic means to resolve it. He ran through the streets of Belley to the bishop's residence, knocked on his door, entered and fell on his knees, avowed his hostile feelings and asked forgiveness. The bishop, thus surprised, received him paternally and embraced him. That was the end of Colin's 'temptation', but not yet of the conflict between them.

Despite their struggle, Devie did not lose his own high regard for Colin. On the contrary, it was precisely because he valued him so highly that he was determined to keep him in his diocese. In the midst of their fiercest tussles, he would still entrust him with important and confidential assignments and even proposed to make him vicar general. The bishop also made several attempts to create him an honorary canon, on one occasion employing the ruse of asking him to bring Monsieur Pichat's canon's cape to the bishop's residence, with the idea of putting it around Colin's shoulders—a manoeuvre that Colin anticipated and foiled by having it sent round by someone else. Colin's avoidance of these appointments should be seen not simply as edifying examples of his refusal to accept honours and dignities, but also and especially as checks to the bishop's game of involving him inextricably in the machinery of the diocese. For his part, Colin never failed in respect and obedience to his bishop and appears to have seen in him a father. He probably recognised his good fortune in working for a great chief, from whom, in due course, he accepted positions of responsibility and leadership. In interacting with Devie, Colin acquired both toughness and the art of diplomacy. All this prepared him for the mission that lay ahead.

When Bishop Devie was on his deathbed in 1852, he asked to see Fr Colin, who came to Belley to make his farewell to his mentor. The dying man gave his blessing to the Society of Mary. He also gave Colin some personal advice and recommendations, not to risk wounding the feelings of others in his dealings with them and not to let his moods run away with him.

Chapter 6
Roman Recognition and Oceania

Towards the end of 1830, Jean-Claude Colin's thoughts began to turn again towards Rome and his vow to lay before the Holy Father the project of the Society of Mary and explain its supernatural origin. Early in the next year, on 2 February 1831, an event occurred in Rome that was to have a determining effect on the fortunes of the Society of Mary. This was the election of a new pope in succession to Pius VIII, who had reigned briefly after the death of Leo XII in 1829. He was Mauro Cappellari and took the name of Gregory XVI. Cappellari was a Camaldolese monk, who combined great personal piety and simplicity of life with deeply conservative policies in both Church and State. As cardinal, he had been Prefect of the Sacred Congregation for the Propagation of the Faith (*de Propaganda Fide,* often simply *Propaganda*)—now 'Evangelisation of Peoples'. In this position he had taken great interest in renewing the missionary endeavour of the Catholic Church, which had been disrupted by the tumults and confiscations of the preceding decades. He was to continue this interest as pope.

When Bishop Devie learned of Colin's desire to go to Rome, he was discouraging. Apparently nothing was done to further the plan for the rest of 1831 and throughout 1832. Things got going again in the following year. It was decided to approach the court of Rome through Cardinal Vincenzo Macchi, whom Colin had dealt with when he was papal nuncio in Paris. In April 1833 Jean-Claude and six other aspiring Marists, including his brother Pierre, and Pierre Chanel, signed a petition to be presented to the Holy Father, which implicitly requested papal approbation of the Society. Other petitions introduced the proposed Constitutions of the Society and asked for indulgences for lay Marist tertiaries. Colin also needed supporting letters from the two dioceses where the Marists were present. He finally obtained from Bishop Devie of Belley and from Archbishop Gaston de Pins, the administrator of Lyons, letters that expressed appreciation of the Marists but stopped short of recommending their approbation by Rome as a pontifical congregation.

By August 1833, Jean-Claude and two companions, Pierre Chanel, from the diocese of Belley, and Antoine Bourdin, from Lyons, were ready to leave for Rome to present the Marist project to the Holy Father. This was the first time in all his forty-three years that Colin had travelled outside France; indeed, it was his first voyage of any length since his two trips to Paris ten years previously. Whatever may have been his breadth of vision—eventually encompassing a good part of the globe—his physical world remained throughout his life extremely limited. He simply had no taste for travel or seeing new places and, like his peasant forebears, he never moved far from home, if he could help it.

The first stop was Lyons, where the Marists laid their projected voyage at the feet of Our Lady of Fourvière and asked her blessing and protection. Next to Marseille, where they found a sailing vessel getting ready to cross the Mediterranean to Civitavecchia, the port of Rome. The boat had a name of good omen, 'Our Lady of Good Help'. She turned out, however, to be a coastal trader, with no accommodation for passengers. The three Marists slept rough on the deck, and Colin and Chanel suffered from seasickness. Storms impeded progress, and the vessel was leaky. Finally, she reached Civitavecchia, only to be told that she would be placed in quarantine. The Marists, however, were allowed to proceed to Rome, where they arrived at the Porta di San Pancrazio on the Janiculum before dawn on 15 September and found lodging in the historic centre near the French national church of Saint Louis des Français. If Jean-Claude experienced any intense emotion on reaching at last the Eternal City, he does not tell us.

The Rome that Jean-Claude Colin saw in 1833 was a much smaller city than today, with a population of scarcely 150,000, contained within its ancient walls, not at all a modern town, even by the standards of the time, almost entirely ecclesiastical and revolving around the papal court. The administration of the Church was not at that time so centred on the Vatican as it is now. The pope usually lived at the Quirinal Palace, where the central offices for the civil government of the Papal States were also located. Audiences were held there, as well as the conclaves to elect a new pope. Other meetings of cardinals might take place at the Quirinal or at the Vatican. The ecclesiastical departments of the Roman curia did not all have their own permanent offices, as they do now, and their officials often worked in the palace of the cardinal who happened to head them at the time.

The three Marists found that they had arrived just as everything was shutting down for the long vacation: Colin already foresaw that he would have to stay on until Christmas. In the mean time, the Marist pilgrims made several calls on Cardinal Macchi and saw other prelates who were still in Rome. They did the usual pilgrim-tourist round. Each day they celebrated Mass at a different church. Like every pilgrim before and since, they bought rosaries, medals and pious books. Like every tourist, they were tired out by the end of the day.

There was one visit, however, still to make, and that the most important, the object in fact of Colin's vow: he had to see the Holy Father and 'open his heart' about the Society of Mary and its rule. Perhaps by this time, he was beginning to perceive the way things really worked in Rome: it was highly unlikely that he would get a chance to have the sort of heart-to-heart talk with the pope that he had imagined. Repeated applications to the papal chamberlain for an audience were, however, met with the response that there were too many audiences already booked for the short time that remained before the pope was due to leave for Castel Gandolfo. Finally Cardinal Macchi obtained an audience for 28 September.

On entering the papal presence, they found before them a short, white-clad figure, undistinguished in appearance, but benevolent in manner, seated on a throne. Following the protocol of the time, they knelt and kissed first his slipper then his hand, after which the pope raised them to their feet and remained standing with them for the rest of the interview. There was a problem of language. Chanel said a few words in Italian, stumbled and halted. Bourdin did no better with Latin. Colin believed that the pope at least understood French and began to speak in that language, but was silenced by a

Steps leading to the papal residence of the Quirinale, Rome, visited by Jean-Claude Colin in 1833.

look. In the end the pope spoke in Latin, while the three Frenchmen replied in their own language. Gregory was well briefed and referred them to the relevant curial officials. The audience was over, except for the pope's final blessing. The three Marists presented the rosaries and medals they had bought on their way to the palace. Then followed an awkward moment as, bowing and backing out of the presence, they tripped on the train of their soutanes and lost their way. The pope called out, 'Turn right' and rang a bell for someone to show his visitors out. At this, Colin turned his back on the pope and bolted for the door, followed by the others. They were out, elated by their experience (afterwards, Jean-Claude saw the funny side of their embarrassing exit). They went immediately to Macchi to tell him all about it; according to Bourdin, he was 'charmed'.

It was now time for Bourdin and Chanel to return to Belley for the school year that would begin in November. Colin accompanied them as far as Loreto, where they venerated the Holy House, believed to have been transported from Nazareth. He then returned to Rome, which would come to life again after the feast of Saint Martin, on 11 November. He passed the winter, living in the Franciscan monastery adjoining the Basilica of the Holy Apostles, meeting cardinals and monsignori who would be involved in the approval of the Society of Mary and its rule, and studying in the *Biblioteca casanate*, a public library attached to the Dominican Priory at Santa Maria sopra Minerva. It was there that he first came across a copy of the Jesuit Constitutions, which were to exercise an important influence on the development of the Marist Constitutions.

The curial prelates whom Colin met were impressed with his sincerity and devotion, but discouraging about his project, which they found 'a little vast', even 'a monstrosity'. The Congregation for Bishops and Regulars met at the Vatican on 31 January 1834 and, on receiving a negative report from Cardinal Castruccio Castracane, decided against the approbation of the Society. As a consolation prize, they did, however, recommend the grant of indulgences requested. There was no point in Colin's staying longer in Rome. He arrived in Belley, sooner than expected, on 21 February. The students celebrated his return to the college-seminary with bell ringing, music, pastries and wine, and the rest of the day off. Shortly afterwards, Bishop Devie allowed him to live at La Capucinière. And there the Marists' affairs remained.

Then, in 1835, things began to change. The Congregation of *Propaganda Fide* decided to set up a missionary vicariate of Western Polynesia in addition to the vicariate of Eastern Polynesia, which had already been entrusted to the Congregation of the Sacred Hearts of Jesus and Mary ('Picpus Fathers'), founded by Pierre Coudrin in 1817. In fact, the new vicariate included on paper also Melanesia and parts of Micronesia. The Catholic mission in the South Pacific was regarded as extremely urgent, as Protestant missionaries, who

Bishop Jean-Baptiste Pompallier, leader of the first mission group to Oceania and pioneer of Catholic establishment in New Zealand.

had had a head start of several decades, were rapidly establishing themselves throughout the region.

The question now was, where to find a head of mission and missionaries. The search led the Congregation of *Propaganda* to Lyons and to Jean-Baptiste-François Pompallier; he had for several years belonged to the group of aspiring Marists—an added attraction, as they might supply the needed missionaries. Overtures began both to Pompallier and to Colin, who, on 10 February 1836, accepted the invitation to staff the new missionary vicariate. In return, he received a papal Brief recognising the priests (only) of the Society of Mary and permitting them to take religious vows and elect a superior general. It was not, however, until 24 September that Colin was elected superior general and he and his companions took the vows of poverty, chastity and obedience. By that time, Pompallier had already been appointed vicar apostolic and consecrated in Rome as titular bishop of Maronea. He presided at the election of Colin, but did not take religious vows, instead making a declaration of adherence to the Society of Mary. At the time, no one, including Colin, seems to have thought it very important that Pompallier was not a professed Marist, and both seem to have regarded him as in all but law a Marist. What it meant, however, was that the head of the new mission in the Pacific did not really belong to the religious congregation to which it had been entrusted.

Pompallier was told in Rome to expect that the Marist missionaries would have their own religious superior and was also told what were the respective spheres of authority of himself, as vicar apostolic, and of the religious superior. Rather to his surprise, Colin delegated to him the powers of religious superior. What was much more important for the future was Pompallier's idea of the authority of the religious superior, which was restricted, he believed, to seeing that the religious kept their rule: everything else concerning the missionaries, including their spiritual and material welfare, fell under the authority of the vicar apostolic. Colin seems at first to have acquiesced in this— after all, he had no other information about the respective powers of religious superior and vicar apostolic than what Pompallier told him, and furthermore, had had only limited experience as a superior. It is, however, important to realise that Colin's delegation to Pompallier was just that, a delegation: there was no idea that the vicar apostolic *as such* should be the religious superior, and Colin could—and eventually did—delegate that authority to others. Here was a further source of later conflict between them.

Chapter 7
Superior General

When Jean-Claude Colin sat at his desk at La Capucinière in Belley for the first time after his election as superior general, perhaps already on the evening of 24 September 1836, he could take stock of his position and of the responsibility that had been laid on him. He had been chosen as the first superior general of a congregation that he had not initiated. Not only that; he found himself at its head against his will. In his own mind, he was a stopgap until one better fitted could take on the leadership. In the meantime, he realised, there was nobody else available to do the job.

Colin's rise to leadership is exceptional and has few parallels. He was prepared to dedicate all his energies to a cause in which he believed, though he had not begun it, undertake important initiatives without desiring office, accept responsibility, though convinced he was not suited to the task his colleagues imposed on him, and looking for the first opportunity to lay it down. He appears to have been without personal ambition or self-interest. His protestations that he was not really the one to lead the Society go well beyond normal hesitations at the prospect of an office that may prove to be beyond one's capacity. They seem to represent what he genuinely thought about himself; he was not being humble or coy, nor is there any need to resort to psychological hypotheses. Reluctance, however, does not necessarily imply lack of commitment. As previously at the Belley college-seminary, Colin, once installed, was not half-hearted in carrying out his charge, but gave himself to it entirely. He was to govern the Society for the next eighteen years. Yet, during that time, he continued to regard his tenure of office as temporary and made several attempts, or at least plans, to resign as superior general, until he was finally allowed to step down in 1854.

Meanwhile, there was work to do. The most important matter was, of course, the despatch of the first missionaries to the Pacific. This was to take place as soon as possible. Thus, the new Society did not have time to organise itself, let alone to prepare itself for a mission to a huge territory on the other side of the world, with a small population scattered over a host of islands, having very different cultures about which not much was known in Europe. If in the beginning there were moments of confusion, hesitation or uncertainty, that is hardly surprising.

At the end of that momentous year 1836, Pompallier, with four Marist priests and three Marist brothers left for the Pacific. These brothers had all been trained by Marcellin Champagnat at the Hermitage. Before leaving Lyons the missionaries had once again climbed the hill to Fourvière to dedicate the new mission to the Blessed Virgin. Their names were inscribed on a scroll to be contained in a votive silver heart; over the years the names of their successors were added.

The harbour of Hokianga where Bishop Pompallier landed in New Zealand, 1838.

After several changes of plan *en route*, Pompallier decided to make his missionary base in New Zealand. On 10 January 1838, the bishop, with one priest and a brother, arrived, after rather more than a year of journeying, at the Hokianga Harbour in the north of the country, where the greater part of the Māori population and also of European settlers were to be found. On the way they had suffered the death of Claude Bret, and left two priests and two brothers on the islands of Wallis and Futuna, where they were the first Christian missionaries. We will leave them all in their new posts, noting only the extreme difficulty of the mission territory that Pompallier and the Marists had taken on, and the precarious existence they often had to lead. We note too the huge distance that separated them from Rome and Lyons and the resulting slowness and hazards of communication—at first, it might take a whole year for a letter from Europe to arrive in New Zealand—and so the transmission of money as well as information and instructions. On the subject of money, the new mission received a start-up grant from both the Congregation of *Propaganda* and the diocese of Lyons. It was, however, to depend for future financial support on the Association for the Propagation of the Faith, whose foundress, Pauline Jaricot, was also a citizen of Lyons, which continued to be, with Paris, the administrative centre of this remarkable lay-led organisation. These funds were channelled to the Pacific through Colin. It was in fact to Lyons that, in 1839, he transferred the mother house of the Society of Mary from Belley. This was a property known as 'Puylata', situated on the slopes above the river Saône and below Fourvière. From the terrace, on a good day, you can see Mont Blanc.

Colin was directly responsible for the Marist priests and coadjutor brothers in Europe, for recruitment and training, for the missionaries in Oceania, also, as their highest authority, for the Marist brothers and for the Marist sisters and laity. Until 1839, he had been governing the Society single-handed. Once installed at Puylata, he constructed a general administration and put in place a regular administrative procedure and practice.

Marcellin Champagnat was a member of this first administration, with special responsibility for the Little Brothers of Mary. Since the middle of 1839, however, his health was a matter of open concern. The question of his succession and of the future government of the Marist brothers was becoming urgent. Colin thought the time had come for the brothers to elect one of their own to run their institute. On 12 October 1839, he was at the Hermitage to preside at the election of the 'brother director general', to be made in accordance with rules that he had drawn up. Brother François Rivat, one of Marcellin Champagnat's first companions, was elected, to direct an institute with 139 brothers in forty-five places in France, as well as those in Oceania. Marcellin, however, still remained 'provincial' of the brothers and continued to correspond with Colin about important questions, such as how to respond to bishops requesting the brothers for their dioceses, which were coming in from all over France—many more than Champagnat could satisfy.

On Ash Wednesday, 4 March 1840, Marcellin was afflicted with a violent pain in the kidneys, which continued until his death. He now set about making his last dispositions. On 18 May, Marcellin dictated his 'spiritual testament'. It is a document that breathes the holiness of the man. Addressing his 'very dear brothers', the dying Champagnat emphasised the unity of the Society of Mary in several branches, under the authority of one superior general.

Portrait of St Marcellin Champagnat in the church of his home parish of Marlhes, Loire.

From 24 to 25 May, Colin was at the Hermitage to say farewell. On 6 June 1840, Marcellin Champagnat died at the age of fifty-one. He was buried two days later. Pierre Colin and other Marist fathers came to the funeral, but not Jean-Claude. Champagnat had been the only one of the original group of equal stature with Colin. The two men had stood together for many years, constantly conferring, not always agreeing, but with a single goal in mind, namely the 'work of Mary'. The provincial of the brothers did not hesitate to express a contrary view to that of the superior general, who not infrequently gave way, although at other times he insisted on Marcellin's compliance. There was an entire confidence between them. For Colin, it was the end of a robust partnership in which, beneath the formalities of the age, genuine appreciation and even affection show through. For the Society of Mary, an age had ended. A great tree had fallen, and the gap was never filled.

The Society of Mary was beginning to grow rapidly. Many who joined were already diocesan priests, who were attracted by the Pacific mission. In 1839 there was only a single entry; but he was a future canonised saint, Pierre-Julien Eymard, priest of the diocese of Grenoble, later founder of the Society of the Blessed Sacrament.

In Oceania, the greater part of manpower and money was invested in New Zealand, which was by far the largest and most populous group of Pacific Islands. Here the Marists ran into a number of problems, in addition to those entailed by distance (which aggravated the others). First, Protestant missionaries had been evangelising the Māori people since 1814—usually with success, although many had not yet embraced Christianity. They and their converts were frequently hostile to the arrival of Catholic missionaries. The Marists also found a large and rapidly growing body of European settlers, a good number of whom, often Irish veterans of the British army, were Catholics; their needs and expectations increasingly competed for the missionaries' attentions with their primary call to evangelise Māori. Two years after the arrival of the French Catholic missionaries, in 1840, the British government established its rule over the whole country, thus thwarting hopes of a French colony in New Zealand. Pompallier and the Marists were apprehensive about how this might affect their position in New Zealand. Finally, friction arose between the bishop and a number of his priests, which eventually involved the superior general.

Pierre Chanel had been left on the island of Futuna, in central Oceania, with Brother Marie-Nizier Delorme; on the neighbouring island of Uvea or Wallis were Pierre Bataillon and Brother Joseph Luzy, who had succeeded, by the end of 1841, in converting practically all the inhabitants. Progress was much slower on Futuna, in fact, almost non-existent. For several years, Chanel succeeded only in baptising some dying babies and a few others. On the other hand, his tireless generosity and goodness won from the local people the name, 'The

Window in the church of Cuet, Montrevel-en-Bresse, home parish of Peter Chanel, depicting his martyrdom in 1841.

man with the good heart'. By April 1841, there were fifteen adult catechumens, one of whom was the son of one of the two kings of the island. His conversion angered his father and led to a plot against Pierre, who was brutally murdered on 28 April. On Futuna too, 'the blood of martyrs was the seed of Christians'; and by 1845 the island was entirely Christian.

The news of Chanel's death did not reach Europe until a year later. Colin's immediate reaction to the news of this second death of a Marist whom he had sent out on mission was one of shock and grief. 'His heart, sensitive in the extreme', an observer recorded, 'was just as moved and overwhelmed by the loss [as it had been by that of Bret]. It was as if he had been struck by lightning.' Then followed the reaction of submission to God's will: 'He went down on his knees, saying to the Lord; 'praise to you! . . . Your holy will be done!'

The superior general announced Chanel's murder to the Society as a martyrdom: 'Let us sing a hymn of praise to Mary our Mother, the Queen of Martyrs. One of her children, our brother, has merited to shed his blood for the glory of Jesus Christ.' Pierre Chanel's violent death as a martyr was recognised by the Church by his beatification in 1889 and canonisation in 1954.

In the years following Chanel's martyrdom, Marists established precarious but ultimately durable missions in Tonga, Fiji, both already evangelised by Methodists, and Samoa. A first attempt to gain a foothold in New Caledonia was defeated, with loss of life, by the hostility of local people; a second also had to be abandoned; a third was successful. The Marist mission in the Solomon Islands and New Guinea proved too difficult and strained the resources of the Society; it was transferred to missionaries of the Milan Missionary Society, but they too could not sustain it. The Marists eventually returned to the Solomons in 1897. The history of the early Marist missions in the south-west Pacific is an heroic story, which has yet to be fully told.

Colin never visited Oceania. He was, nonetheless, deeply implicated in the Marist mission in the South Pacific. Distance sometimes gives a broad perspective. Colin was able—in partnership with the Congregation of *Propaganda Fide* in Rome—to plan for the future development of the Oceania mission, including the erection of new vicariates.

During his time as superior general, Colin sent out fifteen expeditions of missionaries, with a total of one hundred and seventeen

Marists—seventy-four priests, twenty-six Little Brothers of Mary, and seventeen coadjutor brothers. This represents a sacrificial number for what was still a small congregation. Colin was deeply concerned about his men, for whom he felt responsible before God. He insisted on the need for the missionaries to live in community, and more generally on the right of the religious superior to assure their spiritual and temporal welfare. This led him into conflict with Pompallier and later with other missionary bishops, who wanted the missionaries to be entirely under their control, and so caused him to reflect on the respective roles of the ecclesiastical and of the religious superior.

One of the chief ways in which Colin supported the missionaries was as a spiritual guide. Beginning with the first group to leave for Oceania, the superior general gave them a rule of life and a realistic spirituality, which their successors continue to this day.

At the annual retreat in September 1841, Colin made a first attempt to resign—a step that he had been considering for several months, and which he had anticipated by burning his private papers. He believed that the time had come to hand over the government of the Society to another. His confreres did not, however, agree. Colin accepted their decision and settled once again to the task.

Chapter 8
The Oceania Mission

We have arrived at a summit ridge in the life of Jean-Claude Colin, especially in his government as superior general of the Society of Mary. Decisions taken and tendencies confirmed during the spring and summer of the year 1842 shaped events and choices still to come, like the streams that flow down from a watershed in the mountains. For the time being, at least, there was no more talk of resigning. Colin was in harness and had things he wanted to achieve.

In April 1842 the Marists held a 'congregation', which can be regarded as their first general chapter. A number of matters needed to be decided. The principal business was the discussion and approval of a draft text of constitutions, on which Colin had been working for some time. There were also urgent questions concerning Oceania, where relations with Bishop Pompallier were severely strained. These were not, however, discussed on the chapter floor; but Colin commented informally on several of them. An unscheduled act was to accede to a petition of the Marist brothers to declare the permanent union between fathers and brothers in the same Society of Mary and under the one superior general.

The constitutional text approved by the congregation of April 1842 was the most complete yet produced by Jean-Claude Colin. He still did not regard it, however, as the definitive expression of the 'rule'—indeed, the final chapter remained unfinished. Although it was far from being simply a very general outline of the requirements of Marist religious life, Colin refrained from including in it many of the detailed prescriptions that he still regarded as belonging to the rule and which he was to insert into the constitutions of 1872.

Colin had reshaped the body of Marist legislation within a framework, which was basically that of the Society of Jesus. Even a brief comparison reveals, however, that there is no simple correspondence between the contents of the chapters in the two documents. On the one hand, he did not hesitate to make large use of St Ignatius' text, extending to lengthy sections borrowed *verbatim*, notably on the novitiate and on the superior general. On the other hand, he not only adapted his source but also introduced much material that was proper to the Society of Mary and often expressed his own intuitions. So, for example, to the Ignatian portrait of the superior general, with its opening evocation of an army and its pyramidal structure of 'lesser officers' led by a 'major officer', he adds 'motherly care' for the sick, confidence in Mary, opposition to the spirit of the world and to greed for money or possessions. Colin remained fundamentally independent of Ignatius.

His thoughts now turned chiefly to Rome and the voyage he was soon to undertake. He had already written to Cardinal Fransoni, prefect of the congregation of *Propaganda Fide* a letter that revealed the widening rift between Bishop Pompallier and the Marists in New Zealand and their superior general in Lyons. Fransoni was concerned to remedy the quarrel, which jeopardised the whole Pacific mission. He sought at this stage to calm hurt feelings and reconcile the parties. Colin was, however, convinced that much more than soothing words was required from Rome. During his forthcoming visit there, he intended to raise the question of the respective responsibilities of the missionary bishop and the superior regarding the religious to whom the mission was entrusted.

Another topic that had been occupying Colin's mind for some time was that of the reorganisation of the mission in Western Oceania, hitherto a single vast vicariate entrusted to Bishop Pompallier alone. Various plans for a division of the vicariate had already been suggested. Colin now had precise ideas and concrete proposals. He was armed with a six-page 'Overview of the Islands of Western Oceania', intended to serve in fixing the boundaries of the new missions that might be established. It traced the coordinates of the entire area of the south Pacific that formed the vicariate of Western Oceania and identified the major island groups within it: New Zealand; Fiji, Tonga, Samoa, Wallis and Futuna; New Caledonia, the New Hebrides (now Vanuatu) and the Solomons; New Guinea, New Britain, New Ireland,

Mission cross and palm trees, Taveuni, Fiji Islands.

the Admiralty Islands, etc; finally, the Carolinas, distinguishing them from the Marianas, which were already the responsibility of the church in the Philippines. Each group in turn was described, with attention given to climate, natural resources, population and potential for development, and a future ecclesiastical arrangement for the region was proposed. New Zealand, because of its size and population and the interest already shown there by Protestant missionaries, needed two vicariates. A third vicariate would group Fiji, Tonga and Samoa, along with Wallis and Futuna, Rotuma, the Gilbert Islands (now Kiribati) and others. New Caledonia, the New Hebrides and the Solomons should be a fourth vicariate, and New Guinea and its neighbours a fifth. The Micronesian islands of the Carolinas, north of the equator, would make a rich mission field and might also require a vicar apostolic. So well founded were these recommendations that, by the time Jean-Claude Colin retired from the direction of the Society in 1854, all had been or were about to be implemented by Rome.

On 28 May Jean-Claude Colin, with Victor Poupinel as his companion, left Lyons for Marseilles and on to Rome, where they arrived on 2 June. Much had changed in the nine years since his first visit to the Eternal City, and the Rome voyage of 1842 was made under quite different circumstances from that of 1833. Then he had been an obscure priest from a small French diocese seeking papal recognition for a new religious society, which left many sceptical, even if all were impressed by his sincerity and faith. On that occasion he had rather lukewarm recommendations from two bishops and knew no one in Rome except Cardinal Macchi, whom he had met in Paris ten years earlier. Now he was the superior general of a congregation approved by the pope and responsible for a missionary endeavour on the other side of the world. He had about 100 priests directly under his command and was unofficially seen by many as the superior general also of bodies of teaching brothers and sisters, as well as various groups of lay people. For several years, he had been in regular correspondence with Cardinal Fransoni, and was well remembered by other cardinals, notably Castracane, who, though he

Fr Victor Poupinel, secretary and advisor of Jean-Claude Colin during the establishment of the Oceania missions.

continued to oppose the concept of a society with several branches, had come to appreciate and esteem Jean-Claude Colin. Doors would now be thrown open to him. He had become a significant figure in the eyes of the Roman curia.

Poupinel relates that those who were meeting Colin in Rome for the first time were often impressed with his 'look of holiness and simplicity', by his modesty and humility: one even expected that he would be canonised one day and that his statue would occupy the then vacant niche in St Peter's beside that of Alphonsus Liguori. Despite his dislike of the social round, Colin did call on a number of cardinals; he also, of course, had regular business with Fransoni and Castracane. The latter went out of his way to show kindness to Colin and would greet him with marked attention; on one occasion, when he had passed Colin in the street without at first noticing him, he leaned out of his carriage window to wave; on another occasion, when the cardinal himself was on foot, he quickened his pace so as to catch up with him. Colin, of course, walked everywhere, which he found very tiring, until he was prevailed upon by Castracane and others to follow the example of Philip Neri and occasionally take a carriage: there was no need, he was told, to be holier than the saint, who liked to say that in Rome, 'All is vanity, except riding in a carriage'.

As Castracane got to know Colin better, his admiration grew. He told another priest: 'He's the *vir simplex et rectus* (simple and upright man) of whom Holy Scripture speaks [*cf* Job 1:1]. M. Colin is a saint. He has understood his age.'

The most important visit to be made in Rome was, of course, to the Pope, still Gregory XVI. Colin was, however, in no hurry to ask for an audience and did not apply until quite late in his stay in the Eternal City. He confided to Poupinel that he would gladly get out of it if he could, as 'it amounts only to going there to receive compliments from the Holy Father on what the Society is doing for the foreign missions'. He knew by now that he could not discuss business with the pontiff, who would only refer him to the appropriate curial officials. He finally got round to asking for an audience towards the end of July. It was set for 3 August but did not take place until three days later. There was a little awkwardness over protocol, with the pope unwilling to let Colin kiss his slipper and the superior general unwilling to take Gregory's proffered hand. The Pope, it turned out, had again been well briefed about his visitor and talked with him about the Oceania missions, Fr

Chanel, a proposed mission in southern Africa and the protection of the French government. Finally, Colin asked the apostolic blessing for the whole Society. 'Gladly', replied the Holy Father, 'with all my heart, so that it may grow from strength to strength.' It had, after all, been more than a mere courtesy call.

As on the previous occasion, Colin was also a pilgrim and tourist in Rome. As before, he gave himself to study, in particular of canon law. Everyone was congratulating the Society that it already had a martyr in the person of Fr Chanel. He had been told how to proceed in order to introduce the cause of his beatification and wrote back to France asking that as much information as possible should be collected about Chanel's life in France before going to Oceania.

The greatest part of Colin's time was, of course, spent on the business for which he had come to Rome. This involved the preparation and composition of letters and other documents and the consultation of experts, as well as many meetings. Characteristically, it also involved much time spent in prayer. He was now thinking that he would not seek papal approval of his text of constitutions, but rather get advice and reassurance that he was proceeding along the right lines. The difficult point for the Society of Mary was always going to be its multi-branched structure, and especially the incorporation of the teaching brothers, as a largely autonomous body with its own administration, houses and ministries, under the superior general of the fathers. Two experts whom he consulted replied that there would be no problem obtaining papal approbation for the brothers as an independent institute. The stumbling block in the way of getting recognition for the brothers as part of the greater Society of Mary was the opposition previously shown by Cardinal Castracane and his insistence that Rome could approve only the priests.

Colin went to see Castracane, who, as expected, brought forward the earlier decree. The superior general felt, however, that the cardinal did not sufficiently understand the situation in France, where the brothers, still without state recognition, were in a vulnerable position: their union with the priests gave them some protection and an assured status. Once Castracane saw the point, he began looking for a way in which he could get the brothers approved without going back on the existing decree, perhaps as tertiaries. He still, however, retained reservations about the whole idea. He had no doubt that the thing could work as long as Jean-Claude Colin remained superior general.

Beyond that, however, he was less sure and feared future difficulties between fathers and brothers. It would not have escaped him that the brothers were already much more numerous than the fathers, and he foresaw that, one day, they would demand their independence. Colin agreed, especially if future superiors caused trouble for the brothers. Wise legislation might prevent this happening, but you could not legislate for everything, especially for things that might not occur for a long while. In fact, he was not too worried if the branches separated later on; what was more important was the present, when the brothers needed the union with the priests under their superior. Now, it seems, the 'branches' were beginning to be for him less a matter of principle than of practical convenience.

There were also, of course, important discussions between Colin and Cardinal Fransoni regarding Oceania. Colin maintained that, to settle the differences in New Zealand, the legitimate authority of a religious superior over subjects staffing a missionary vicariate had to be made clear. The prefect of *Propaganda* eventually agreed and invited Colin to set out what he thought a decree of the Roman congregation should contain. He asked for four things: to establish a provincial in New Zealand, who would represent the superior general of the Society of Mary and, without prejudice to the rights and jurisdiction of the vicar apostolic and together with him, would 'watch over each of the missionaries'; in case of need, to be able to withdraw and replace a missionary, giving prior notice to the congregation of Propaganda; to require that the missionaries should not ordinarily be placed in isolation; to recall one of the missionaries every four or five years in order to report to *Propaganda* and the superior of the Society all that concerned the welfare of the mission and each missionary. The congregation agreed to these provisions; but, in a later version of its decree, which was to apply more widely than just the Marist missions in the Pacific, added a fifth article, to the effect that communications between the vicar apostolic and Rome were to pass through the superior general. Colin had not asked for this and foresaw that it would lead to further difficulties. This turned out to be the case, and, in 1846, Rome rescinded the entire decree.

The next item on Colin's agenda during his visit to Rome in 1842 was a beginning of the restructuring of the Catholic mission in the southwest Pacific. He successfully petitioned Cardinal Fransoni for the erection of a new vicariate of Central Oceania, to include Tonga,

Fiji, Samoa as well as Wallis and Futuna. The superior general made a case for taking urgency, to forestall further growth of the Protestant presence in Fiji, Tonga, and Samoa.

By early August 1842 Jean-Claude Colin had concluded his business in Rome and was hoping to be able to leave with Victor Poupinel on the evening of 15 August, feast of the Assumption of Our Lady. In the mean time, he had contracted malaria—a common scourge in Rome in those days—and needed a doctor, who prescribed the usual purge but, to greater effect, quinine. Colin was sufficiently impressed by the severity of his illness to ask Poupinel to send for his confessor if he got any worse, and to give instructions about what to do with his papers.

In the end, they were able to leave Rome on the evening of 28 August. Poupinel was concerned about how well the superior general would stand up to the journey to France. Colin arrived in Lyons completely exhausted and exclaimed: 'Ah! It's time. I can't go any further.' The fever had recurred, and he took to his bed.

Chapter 9
The Society in Europe

As the Society grew, it was becoming urgent to have constitutions in a final form approved by the Holy See. Colin in the end had not asked for approval of his text of 1842. During the following years, he continued to work on the rule. He was also committed to writing constitutions for the sisters and for the lay branch, and, at one time, also for the Marist brothers. From this point, he began to give thought to resigning as superior general, in order to devote himself fully to the task of writing constitutions; he submitted his resignation to the chapter of 1845, which, however, refused to accept it, but gave him time off from the government of the Society.

1848 was again a year of revolution in France and widely in Europe. In the city of Lyons, the fall of King Louis-Philippe on 24 February was the signal for bands of workers, especially silk weavers, the principal industry of Lyons, to roam the streets, enter religious houses and break any looms they found. Their grievance was that these houses, often orphanages and similar institutions, employed the unpaid labour of their residents and so kept the other workers' wages low.

Staircase in the General House of Puylata, Lyons. Jean-Claude lived at Puylata as superior-general from 1839 to 1852.

Marists at Puylata, though they had no silk looms, expected their house too to be invaded and feared violence and pillage. Colin had summed up the situation and once again showed the same cool head that had maintained order at the Belley school in 1831. On the evening of the 26th, he told the community what in fact had been happening in Paris and Lyons—the best way of countering rumours and speculations and calming people down. So far the only violence offered had been towards the silk looms, not to the religious themselves. The Marists, he said, should expect visitors that night, and he announced how they were to be received. A father and two brothers would keep watch and immediately show 'the envoys of the Republic' into the refectory, where they would find bread, fruit, cheese and wine—he had ordered plenty to be brought up from the cellars. A stroke of the bell would tell each Marist to be ready, with his lamp lit; they were to receive those who came to inspect their rooms—presumably looking for looms—'with great politeness'. The suggestion had been made to remove a conspicuous statue of Our Lady: 'I shall certainly not do so, and what would the blessed Virgin say? She is our guardian.' Besides, the sight of her would have a good effect on those who came.

The expected visit occurred. Armed workers enrolled in the National Guard were received by Colin and a companion, ate and drank all they wanted, asked for a certificate of their good behaviour and left. They were obviously pleased with their reception at the Marists' and returned nine times over the next two days. Finally, on the 28th, the house was officially required to supply food to the revolutionaries, but a guard was posted at the door to prevent further incursions. As a result, the Marists were able to continue with their normal duties, instead of going into hiding, as other religious priests had done.

The immediate crisis had been surmounted. Colin—despite his personal preference for the old Bourbon monarchy—believed that he and the Marists could get along even with a republic. He realised, however, that a great change was coming about in France, which would not be without important consequences for the Church and for the Society of Mary. On 11 March 1848, the provisional commissary of the republic in Lyons proclaimed the dissolution of all unauthorised religious congregations (which included the Marists). This decree was not put into effect, but four days later, fearing the forced dispersal of religious and the confiscation of their property, Colin arranged for Puylata to be leased to friends for three years and relocated most of the Marists who were there and in other large (and therefore conspicuous) communities; he told those in Paris to be ready to leave the capital if necessary. He also redoubled his insistence that the Marists should not draw hostile attention to themselves, but were to be literally 'hidden and unknown in this world'. Instead of openly opposing 'wrong' ideas, such as the communism that was beginning to be prevalent, Marists should be working for the salvation of those who professed them.

In the event, order was soon restored, and a conservative Second Republic installed, which soon transformed itself into the Second Empire under Napoleon III. Even so, the 1848 revolution disrupted more than one project, such as the plan to hold a 'second novitiate' for those who had already spent four or five years in the ministry.

Colin's remarks betray at times a deepening pessimism about the period in which the Society was living. He never proclaimed the imminent end of the world; but it seems that privately he believed it might be close. That, however, was no cause for fear or dismay, as Mary had promised to be the support of the Church at the end; this was, in fact, the very time when her Society would come into its own: 'Mary will make use of us, her sons'. He laid a growing emphasis on the need for faith and prayer, which 'alone can convince people's minds, enlighten their intellect and touch their hearts'. The Society of Mary was 'a pre-eminently active body'; but it would achieve nothing 'unless we unite in ourselves the man of prayer and the man of action'.

Despite his constant preoccupation with Oceania, Colin also presided over a period of growth for the Society of Mary in France. Preaching continued to be a major apostolate. The work of parish missions continued. This was complemented by other forms of preaching, such as special series of sermons and instructions at Advent, Lent or Corpus Christi. The giving of retreats to priests, seminarians or religious became an increasingly important activity. In 1838 a new work emerged, when the Marists were invited to take charge of the pilgrimage shrine of Our Lady of Verdelais, near Bordeaux (this was also the occasion of moving for the first time beyond the dioceses of Lyons and Belley). In 1846 and 1847 Colin accepted two more pilgrimage centres, Our Lady of Grace, at Rochefort-du-Gard in southern France, and Our Lady of Bon-Encontre, near

Agen to the south-east of Bordeaux. During the high seasons of these shrines the Marists were occupied with the spiritual and even the temporal care of the pilgrims. At other times they were free to go out on parish missions. At Verdelais and Agen parishes were attached to the sanctuaries. Fr Colin was, however, resolutely opposed to the Marists taking on regular parishes, which he saw as contrary to their missionary vocation.

Colin increasingly promoted education as a major work of the Society of Mary. The Marists finally left the Belley college-seminary in 1845. In that same year, however, a new

The shrine of Our Lady of Verdelais, south-western France, accepted by Jean-Claude Colin and the Marists in 1838.

college was started at Valbenoîte (Loire), in buildings that had once belonged to a Benedictine abbey. Marists had in fact been there since 1831, acting as curates for the parish priest, who had bought the site and intended to leave it to the Society. On his death in 1844, Colin decided to establish a boarding school there, which soon had all the usual classes and around ninety pupils. Disputes arose, however, over the way the property had been left, and a court judgment decided against the Society. The superior general then decided to accept the invitation from the town authorities of Saint-Chamond, which is close to the Hermitage, to take over the municipal college, to which he transferred the establishment at Valbenoîte. A similar invitation saw the Marists come to the small town of Langogne (Lozère), where they built up the run-down college, then handed it back to the diocesan clergy.

Toulon (Var) was and still is an important French naval base. In 1845 the Marists had established a residence for home missionaries at nearby La-Seyne-sur-Mer, and the idea took hold of setting up a secondary school there. It was not, however, until 1849 that they received the authorisation to establish a school, which began in a very small way but gradually grew until, by 1854, it had 140 pupils, mostly sons of naval officers.

The last two schools begun in Fr Colin's time as general were at Brioude (Haute-Loire) in 1853–1854, and at Montluçon (Allier) also in 1853.

Another important educational work that the Society embraced while Colin was general was to staff diocesan major seminaries, where candidates for Holy Orders studied theology and were prepared for the priesthood. The first of these was at Moulins (Allier, in 1847), which was followed by Digne (Alpes-de-Haute-Provence, in 1849) and Nevers (Nièvre, in 1852). The Marists also took on the direction of the minor seminary at Digne in 1853.

Naturally, at this stage of its history, most who came to the Society of Mary were French nationals. It is, however, interesting to note that, even then, its membership was starting to become more diverse, with as many as nineteen coming from Savoy, and so, at this period, not French nationals but citizens of the kingdom of Sardinia-Piedmont. There was also a handful representing other European countries.

Throughout Fr Colin's time as general, suggestions and offers had come in to establish a Marist presence in either England or Ireland. The special attraction here was, of course, the possibility to learn English and even recruit native English-speakers for the Pacific missions, which included British as well as French territories. Colin had not, however, felt that the limited resources of the Society would allow it to accept such offers.

St Anne's, Spitalfields, in London's East End, UK, established by Jean-Claude Colin in 1850 for Marists to work among Irish immigrants.

In 1850, however, the Society of Mary made its first European fondation outside France. This was in London, a city already familiar to many Marists in transit to or from Oceania. At the end of March of that year, Bishop Nicholas Wiseman, vicar apostolic of the London district and soon, with the restoration of the Catholic hierarchy in England and Wales, to become cardinal archbishop of Westminster, approached the Marists about the possibility of opening a house in Spitalfields, in the East End of London; there they were to work among the Irish immigrants, who had come in vastly larger numbers after the recent famine, and whose needs overtaxed the English church. They were currently being cared for by Joseph Quiblier, whom Colin knew from Rome, when he had been superior of the Sulpicians of Montreal, and it was presumably he who had suggested the Marists to Wiseman and acted as intermediary.

Quiblier soon came in person to Puylata, and Colin agreed to send three priests and two brothers. There was no Catholic church or presbytery at Spitalfields. The Marists would have to build them, and Colin asked for help from the Association for the Propagation of the Faith. The fruit of these negotiations was a Marist missionary presence in the East End of London, caring for successive waves of new immigrants, which lasted until recent times.

Chapter 10
The Future of the Society

Colin was thinking also of the future shape of the Society. More and more he felt that Rome's constant opposition to the approval of a multi-branch Society could mean that it was not, after all, according to the will of God. He began to prepare the Marist brothers for separation from the fathers. A key moment in this development was State approval of the brothers as a teaching congregation in 1852, which meant they had no further need of the 'umbrella' provided by the fathers. By 1854, the year in which Colin resigned as superior general, the brothers were fully independent.

If the separation from the brothers was in the event painless, that from the sisters was anything but that. In a nutshell, Colin believed that the Marist sisters also needed to become a fully independent congregation, of diocesan right pending pontifical approbation. This was a defensible position. Rather less easy to understand is his insistence that they had to stop calling themselves Marist sisters and adopt the name of 'Religious of the Holy Name of Mary'. Jeanne-Marie Chavoin, no longer superior of the sisters, eloquently argued that, whatever their canonical status, it was God's will that the sisters remain a branch of the Society. There were many complicating factors in all this, including the rise to positions of leadership in the congregation of a new generation of sisters, whose ideas were not identical with those of the foundress. Finally, Colin lost patience with Jeanne-Marie and, for a time, broke off relations. It was a sad end to a long and once deep friendship. The Marist sisters, in the event, kept their name, adopted constitutions written by Fr Colin and eventually became a congregation of pontifical right.

Thus far we have had little to say about the third branch of the Society, as originally planned, for lay members. In fact Colin was only occasionally involved directly with it. An important event in the history of the lay branch was his appointment, towards the end of 1845, of Pierre-Julien Eymard as its director. Eymard's direction of the Third Order of Mary was decisive in its history, both for the growth in numbers of tertiaries and the formation of particular groups catering for different categories of persons, as also for the orientation he gave them. On 8 December 1846, he received into the Marist Third Order its most illustrious member, Jean-Marie Vianney, the holy curé of Ars. The rule he composed in 1847 was in the classic tradition of 'third orders', such as those of the Franciscans, Dominicans and Carmelites, namely of lay people who not only were closely associated with the religious but also lived a kind of mitigated religious life in the world, with much emphasis on prayer and the interior life.

This conception of the lay branch was in contrast with the very different vision of the 'Confraternity of Faithful of Both Sexes Living in the World', which Colin had sketched in the *Summarium* of 1833. This was potentially open to all Catholics and prescribed only a few simple prayers and pious practices. And yet—at least at this stage—he did not protest against Eymard's rule. Perhaps he was merely leaving things to the man he had appointed; and in any case, despite his declared intentions, he had not yet written the rule for the Third Order. It is also possible that prudence and experience played their part in this change of direction. The 1833 idea—of an organisation open to all and with a universal mission, which would be subject to the Marist superior general—had not commended itself to Cardinal Castracane and the Roman curia, who feared that it might be perceived by civil rulers as subversive. Authorities of both church and state would be much more comfortable with a traditional third order along familiar lines. Colin's earlier idea on the laity—like so many others concerning the Society—could bide its time.

Regarding the Society's works, Colin was becoming increasingly pessimistic about the future of the Marists in the Pacific. The situation in New Zealand was resolved by the creation of two dioceses, one of which (Auckland) was to remain with Bishop Pompallier, while the Marists were to withdraw to the other (Wellington). The question of the relations between the ecclesiastical and the religious superiors in missionary vicariates was finally settled in 1851, but in a direction completely opposite to Colin's ideas: henceforth, in a missionary territory entrusted to a religious order or congregation, the head of mission was to be regarded *ex officio* as also the religious superior. Colin's experiences of difficulties with missionary bishops led him even to question the suitability of religious to staff a missionary vicariate.

In any case, he appears to have felt that the human cost of the Marist effort in Oceania was too high. Of the missionaries whom he sent out, twenty-one had died, of violence or disease, before 1854. It was time at least to pause and take stock. After 1849 he sent no more missionaries to Oceania, although he continued to support those who were there. Missionary expeditions were resumed by his successor.

At the same time as he was re-thinking the Marist mission in Oceania, Colin was moving the Society decisively into education, which he saw as equally 'mission territory'. As we have seen, he established new communities, both in existing schools that the Society was asked to staff and in new foundations. In 1848 the annual retreat was followed by a study week on education, which attested to the growing importance of this work in the priests' branch. In the following year, he convoked the superiors of the educational establishments to meet and work out a common study plan for Marist colleges.

The years after 1848 also saw the emergence of a new Marist venture. In 1841, as he was waiting in the courtyard of the Belley college for the coach that was to take him back to Lyons, Colin revealed to his companions that he was thinking of a contemplative branch. The idea seems to have originated with some of the lay tertiaries of Lyons, who wanted to lead a life of prayer and recollection. Colin was sympathetic; indeed, he would like such a life for himself. He had discussed the project with the bishop of Belley, who approved. A property was available, and he was under pressure to establish a type of contemplative community there. It

The retreat of Marcellange in the diocese of Moulins established by Jean-Claude Colin in 1842 as a place of rest and study for Marist missioners.

would live under a much less demanding rule than that of the Trappists or Carthusians. The new community was established at Marcellange (Allier) in June 1842. Two years later, the house was closed; but Colin did not abandon the idea.

The 'chateau' of La Neylière, Rhône, acquired in 1850 where Jean-Claude Colin lived and worked after his resignation as superior-general.

By 1850 Colin had found a more suitable property, called 'La Neylière', in the Monts du Lyonnais. This house was to occupy much of Colin's time and attention in the coming months and years. In the mean time, the project had somewhat evolved, from being a 'mitigated Trappist monastery' essentially for laymen, to one in which Marist fathers would also be involved. A further important change came from outside the Society. Adoration of the Eucharist had long been a central devotion in Catholic life. In Paris and elsewhere a movement was taking shape to organise perpetual adoration, and Marist father Antoine Bertholon was heavily involved in it. He became the spiritual director of Mother Marie-Thérèse (Théodelinde) Dubouché, foundress of the Soeurs de l'Adoration Réparatrice (Sisters of Reparative Adoration). Other Marists also got to know her.

Meanwhile, during the procession of the Blessed Sacrament in Lyons on the feast of Corpus Christi in 1845, Pierre-Julien Eymard experienced a strong attraction to make Jesus in the Eucharist the focus of his priestly ministry. In January 1849 he was in Paris, where he met the Eucharistic group and returned to Lyons with ideas for promoting Eucharistic devotion among the Marists. In the same year, Cardinal de Bonald asked the Marist fathers to look after the devotion of nocturnal adoration in the city. Also in 1849, Mother Marie-Thérèse had an ecstasy in which she saw priests in adoration and understood that they were Marists.

At the annual retreat in September 1850, Colin was able to speak about the new property of La Neylière acquired 'in the interests of the Society and for other very powerful motives that concern the glory of God and the good of souls'. He went into some detail about the purpose of the house and his hopes for it and exclaimed: 'Ah, if only this house could be imbued with the spirit given by St. Francis de Sales to the convent of the Visitation!'

By May 1852, after extensive alterations had been completed to the house, Colin felt able to set up a community at there. In the course of the inaugural retreat, he spoke several times about the new work, giving details of the rule to be observed. By now, he was not just thinking of a single house, but of a larger 'work', even a 'new branch' of several houses under the authority of the superior general.

Colin also set out the two purposes he intended the house to fulfil: first, to offer a 'refuge' to many souls for whom the world was full of dangers and who wanted to give themselves sincerely to God— for this reason it would 'probably' be placed under the patronage of Our Lady of Pity or Compassion; second, to offer active members of the Society of Mary a place of retreat where they could renew their zeal and where they could prepare for death at the end of their career. At

Statue of the Blessed Virgin near the rooms of Jean-Claude Colin, La Neylière.

this stage, it appears, Eucharistic adoration was to be an important part of the life at La Neylière, but not its sole or main purpose.

On 24 July 1853, Colin blessed the chapel of Our Lady of Compassion at La Neylière. At the annual retreat of that year, he spoke at length about the house. By now he wished it to be a 'house of prayer where there would be perpetual adoration'. That was not the only new development in his thinking. He envisaged a situation where one part of the Society would be engaged in preaching and going after sinners to convert them, while the other part would constantly 'raise its hands to heaven' to bring grace upon the missionaries. Not those who pursued the sinners, but those who prayed would be the real missionaries.

Colin shared with Dubouché his hopes and intentions for the Marist Eucharistic work as well as showing interest in hers. Towards the end of 1853, he could envisage that 'the priests who occupy themselves in France with the work of adoration of the Blessed Sacrament' might one day 'form a corporation uniquely occupied with [this] work, almost on the same plan as the sisters of the Reparation'. For the time being, however, he was not looking beyond La Neylière. He seemed to be taking a very wide view of 'the Eucharistic work' in the various manifestations in which it presented itself in France, among priests, sisters and laypeople, seeing it as having 'several branches and spreading on all sides', without one branch depending upon another. His idea, he told Dubouché, was to 'encourage all these works, which tend towards the same goal, to repair the outrages done to our Lord', and he advised her to follow the same line. It is clear that he was very far from wanting to place himself at the head of this manifold 'work', or to bring its various 'branches' under the aegis of the Society of Mary. In fact, the Marists were to remain 'unknown' and did not want his or their name to be pronounced.

As the year 1854 began, therefore, the Marist Eucharistic project was still 'work in progress', with Colin—cautious as ever—refusing to 'go too fast' and wary of getting drawn into grandiose schemes. In January and again in March (twice), he had occasion to write to Eymard, but made no mention of La Neylière or of the Eucharistic work. The evolution of their respective ideas seems to have been a case of parallel development. In any case, he told Dubouché, La Neylière 'is still the favourite work for me, I desire nothing so much as to end my days at the foot of the holy altars', and he hoped that God would soon grant him 'freedom'.

Chapter 11
'Father Founder'

From 1851 Jean-Claude Colin was planning his resignation. Ever since his election as superior general on 24 September 1836 he had been waiting for the moment when his office could be entrusted to other hands and had already made two attempts, in 1841 and 1845, to resign. On both occasions his confreres had not permitted this: no doubt they had a higher opinion than he of his ability to govern them. He had always suffered the physical and emotional effects of stress, and now felt that his strength was failing. Besides, he needed to complete the work on the constitutions. This time his confreres were inclined to agree with his own estimate of his fitness to continue and seem to have felt that it was time for a change at the top. Some, however, feared that Colin's departure from office could lead to division in the Society. It was also a question whether, once he was no longer superior general, Colin would still have the authority to give the Society its constitutions. Jean-Claude, on the other hand, believed that this authority came from on high and was independent of elected office.

Before he could resign, Colin needed to prepare the legal ground. The Society of Mary lacked any accepted and approved procedure for electing a superior general, which would, of course, have been laid down in its constitutions. So Colin had to devise an electoral process that was formally accepted by the members of the Society and expressly approved by Rome. At last everything was ready, and, at a chapter that met in Lyons on 5 May 1854, Jean-Claude Colin laid down the office of superior general of the Society of Mary.

The Society that Colin handed over now numbered 211 priests and twenty-three coadjutor brothers in Europe, organised in two

71

provinces. The larger, Lyons, comprised—besides the mother house at Puylata and the new venture at La Neylière—a novitiate at Lyons, a scholasticate at Belley, a third novitiate-scholasticate, five colleges (Brioude, Langogne, Montluçon, Saint-Chamond, La Seyne), three major diocesan seminaries (Digne, Moulins, Nevers) and a minor seminary (Digne), four residences of parish missionaries (Moulins, Riom, Rochefort, Toulon), three chaplaincies to Marist brothers (including the Hermitage) and a chaplaincy to Marist sisters.

The province of Paris was smaller. Its novices and scholastics were trained in the province of Lyons and it had at this date no colleges. There were five large communities: Paris, Bon-Encontre (missions), Valenciennes (missions), Verdelais (Marian sanctuary, parish, missions) and London.

Of the missionaries whom Colin had sent out to the Pacific, fifty-three (forty-four priests and nine brothers) were still in Oceania; of the sixty-eight who were no longer there, twenty-one had died on mission, some of them by violence, and others had returned to Europe or departed. In New Zealand, the Marists had left the fourteen mission stations they had started in what was now the diocese of Auckland, but had four in the new diocese of Wellington. In Central Oceania there were mission stations on Futuna and Wallis, three in Fiji, three in Samoa, and two in Tonga. In New Caledonia there were four stations. Finally, there was a mission supply house in Sydney, New South Wales.

Colin had also turned down many invitations from France and elsewhere, which he felt the resources of the Society did not allow him to accept. For similar reasons he could not, he believed, accept calls to missions other than Oceania; one, to southern Africa, he hesitated over for a long time before finally refusing it.

Colin's achievement lay in taking on a religious enterprise that he had not initiated and bringing it to the point where it was securely established. When he became central superior in 1830, the continued existence of the Society of Mary was in doubt. During the next twenty-four years, he guided—not without difficulties and contradictions—the inchoate groups of priests, brothers and sisters who regarded themselves as its branches towards maturity and recognition, eventually as independent religious congregations. For this reason, he eminently deserved the title of 'Father Founder', which was soon bestowed on him.

On 10 May the general chapter chose Julien Favre as second superior general of the Society of Mary. Aged forty-one years, he was a native of Hotonnes (Ain) and was ordained priest of the diocese of Belley in 1836. Shortly afterwards he entered the newly recognised Society of Mary and began to teach theology at La Capucinière. He remained at this post until, in 1852, Colin appointed him provincial of Lyons and thus effectively the second in the Marist hierarchy. Given that by now Colin was preparing to depart, Favre might be regarded as his designated successor. In any case, the chapter elected him on the first round of voting.

A comment attributed to Denis Maîtrepierre after Julien Favre succeeded Jean-Claude Colin as superior general of the Society of Mary may be taken as summarising—at the risk of caricature—the contrast between the two men: 'We had a founder; now, we have an organiser.' Such a remark can, of course, be taken in more than one way: it could express regret that the days of inspiration and innovation were over; it could also express satisfaction that they had given way to normality and predictability. Maîtrepierre, who had for a time been closely associated with Colin as his second-in-command, realised that a profound change had taken place. There may have been a tinge of regret for what had passed; there could be little doubt, however, that, on the whole, he—and probably many Marists—were content, even relieved, to settle down to a new phase of consolidation and regular growth under a man of method and order, in other words, an 'organiser'.

In many religious orders and congregations—indeed in many other types of organisation—the transition from the founding person and generation to the next is notoriously delicate, as the new people want to move ahead, sometimes in ways that depart more or less notably from those previously laid down. It is hardly surprising that the passage from Colin to Favre was not without difficulty and gave rise to hurts and incomprehension on both sides. That the resulting contention remained within the Society and was resolved without schism or scandal is in great part due to the restraint shown by the two men and to their common devotion to the Society and shared desire to place its interests ahead of personal considerations.

Colin had left office without resolving the question whether 'the Marist Fathers of the Blessed Sacrament' (as he often called them) should become a work outside the Society of Mary, or whether it should be a branch within it, and, if the latter, what precisely would be its relationship to the parent body. These were questions that were arousing disquiet among members of the Society. By ceasing to be superior general he had forfeited his right to settle them. Soon a crisis was developing over the involvement of Marists, especially Colin himself, in the Eucharistic work. Favre moved to signify his 'formal opposition' to the enterprise of La Neylière, from which Colin inferred that the Eucharistic work would have to be juridically separate from the rest of the Society of Mary. He did not seem to think, however, that this prevented him from having anything more to do with it. By August 1855, Julien Favre decided that the time had come for an explicit intervention. We have no direct record of what passed between the two men: the outcome was that, in obedience to his successor, Colin renounced his plan for a contemplative/Eucharistic community at La Neylière, which he had so much at heart.

Nevertheless, he continued to show interest and support for others, both inside and outside the Society, who were involved in Eucharistic projects. One of these was Pierre-Julien Eymard, whose affairs too were moving towards a moment of decision. In several meetings between them, Favre made his views clear. He esteemed the Eucharistic work in itself, but regarded it as something external to the Society of Mary. He also valued Eymard highly and wished to keep him in the Society. For that reason, he wanted him to withdraw from the Eucharistic work.

Eymard, however, believed that his Eucharistic mission took priority. On 14 May 1856 he was dispensed from his vows in the Society of Mary and moved to Paris, to begin the Society of the Blessed Sacrament. On his acceptance by the archbishop of Paris, he wrote to Favre asking him to

The desk in the study of Jean-Claude Colin in La Neylière.

continue his friendship towards him and, in any correspondence with Rome, to speak only of the 'work' and not of his own 'unworthiness'. Favre assured him that 'the separation that has taken place between us will not prevent us from loving one another always in the hearts of Jesus and Mary'. He informed the Marists of Eymard's move in terms of great generosity, praying that he might 'make known, loved and glorified more and more our Lord in the sacrament of his love, and we will rejoice with all our heart.'

One of the reasons that Colin had resigned as superior general was to write constitutions for the Society of Mary. He came to Belley in November 1855 and began work on those of the sisters and also on regulations for the coadjutor brothers. He did not know that, by now, Julien Favre had begun to write 'Fundamental Rules' for the fathers. This was the beginning of a protracted crisis, which later blew up into proportions that threatened the unity of the Society of Mary.

Favre later told Colin that he had composed his rule 'rather despite myself, giving way to the pressing demands of the council and of a very great number of my confreres'. This explanation did not proceed simply from a wish to excuse himself or shift responsibility on to others. The new administration felt the pressing need of an authoritative rule for the government of Marist houses and works. Favre could not, like Colin, assure Marists that such or such a point was 'in the rule' or 'would be in the rule'. Potential candidates for the Society who asked to see its constitutions were 'astonished and even disappointed' to be told that there were as yet no definitively written rules. They were in effect being invited to commit themselves to something undefined. For all these reasons, it is not hard to see why Favre's council should have pressed him to provide the Society—not indeed with definitive constitutions, which they still hoped to receive from Colin—but with an authoritative interim collection of its basic rules, which would guide its internal government and could be given to candidates and novices. Favre and an assistant worked quickly and efficiently. By 6 January 1856 they had produced a text of *Regulae fundamentales Societatis Mariae ex illius constitutionibus excerptae*, which Favre published on 2 February following. The title expresses an intention to compile only 'fundamental rules', which were 'excerpted' from the Society's constitutions. To the uninitiated, they might have seemed simply a vade mecum extracted from a text presumed to exist, which had been approved.

The real question is not why Favre and his advisers produced such a text—the logic is plain—but why they acted without telling Colin. Better still, why did the new superior general not simply offer Colin help to complete the work on the fathers' constitutions? Would he not, by so doing, have avoided much trouble for himself and the Society of Mary in both the shorter and the longer term? It seems that Favre's decision not to approach Colin—a decision certainly made on the advice of his nearest councillors and perhaps instigated by them—was motivated by experience and observation of the increasing difficulty of working with him. Better, then, to brave his wrath after the event than to engage in what would probably be protracted dealings that bore no promise of a useful result.

When Colin was presented with a copy of Favre's 'Fundamental Rules' in February 1856, he needed to do no more than read the first page to see how, despite claiming that they were 'excerpted from the constitutions', the new superior general was in fact—perhaps without fully realising it—operating some quite radical departures. Was it still the same Society?

Did Colin ever think at this time of following Eymard, with whom he had long conversations in Lyons in March 1856? This was later asserted. If so, he might have been inclined to feel that he would be justified by the new direction in which Julien Favre seemed to be taking the Society of Mary. If he no longer recognised in it the society that he had given his life for, might it not be better to make a clean break and join the new society that he had called 'the left door' of his heart? In the event, we know, he remained in the society that was 'the right door' of his heart.

Favre submitted his 'Fundamental Rules' to the Roman Congregation for Bishops and Regulars in April 1856. The congregation passed them on to a consulter, who made a number of comments. One of these was to point out that, since constitutions of the Society of Mary had never been approved, it was therefore inappropriate to declare in the title that these fundamental rules had been 'excerpted from [the Society's] constitutions'. Favre set about further revising the text, now to be called simply 'Fundamental Rules of the Society of Mary'.

Colin felt that he had been bypassed. The years that followed, from the mid-1850s to the mid-1860s, were largely years of retirement and silence. He took no part in the affairs of the Society and did not attend chapters or common retreats. The only public activity in which he was regularly engaged was for the Marist sisters: he continued to accompany them and to work on their constitutions. He was gradually ageing. Bouts of illness were becoming more frequent and left him progressively weaker. He still continued to travel to familiar places, but tended to spend more and more time at La Neylière. His life there took on a regular pattern, which we are able to observe through the eyes of companions and visitors. He now had more time to keep in touch with his relations, especially remaining siblings and a nephew and two nieces who were Marists. He also continued to correspond with Mother Marie-Thérèse Dubouché until her death in August 1863.

Meanwhile, on 13 July 1856, Jean-Claude suffered the loss of his brother Pierre, whose life had been so bound up with his own. He was with him at Puylata when he died. Pierre Colin lived necessarily somewhat in the shade of his younger brother. He was, nonetheless, an important and much-loved figure in the Society, in which he was known by the title of 'Father Director', which he had borne since his days as spiritual director of the Belley college. He had played a significant part alongside Jean-Claude in trying to establish the Society in the early days at Cerdon, and, indeed, as parish priest, had, at least formally, taken the lead in several official acts. He could be regarded as co-founder of the Marist sisters, since he was the one who had known Jeanne-Marie Chavoin and brought her and Marie Jotillon to Cerdon, where he continued to be their guide and protector. He remained one of Jean-Claude's closest collaborators—a position that was not always easy, even for the superior's sibling. Jean-Claude felt Pierre's loss deeply.

Two years later, on 30 June 1858, Jeanne-Marie Chavoin died at Jarnosse (Loire). Jean-Claude had been meaning to go and see her, but never got around to it. He was now the sole survivor of the heroic years of Cerdon and Belley, when she and the Colin brothers supported one another in their plans and work for the Society of Mary. Despite their recent differences, the relationship between Jean-Claude and Jeanne-Marie had once been close and deep. Perhaps that explains the note of bitterness in his reaction to her refusal to go along with his later ideas about the sisters. In any case, here was another irreparable gap in the circle of old friends and comrades-in-arms.

At the beginning of 1860 the frosty relations between Jean-Claude Colin and Julien Favre started to thaw. The superior general sent New Year's greetings to his predecessor. Colin replied graciously, assuring his successor of his constant prayers for him and for the Society.

In the middle of that year, on 15 June 1860, the Holy See approved Favre's rule, now called 'Constitutions of the Priests of the Society of Mary', for a trial period of six years. Colin concluded that he had been 'relieved of the mission to produce constitutions in the eyes of God and the Society', and had no further duty than to prepare for death.

Not all Marists, however, agreed with this assessment. A growing number felt that only Fr Colin had the right to compose the definitive constitutions of the Society. A general chapter was called for 1866, which Fr Favre urged his predecessor to attend, in order to 'put the seal of your wisdom and authority on your own work', and asked pardon for 'anything that may have distressed' him'. When the chapter opened on 5 June, Jean-Claude Colin was there seated beside Julien Favre. The talk and the mood was all of unity and harmony. The (slightly anticipated) Golden Jubilee of Colin's priestly ordination was solemnly celebrated. Most significantly, the chapter entrusted to him 'the redaction of our rules'. Everyone, including Colin himself, assumed that this meant taking Favre's text as a basis and revising it. Meanwhile, the Holy See was asked to extend the trial period for a further six years.

Progress, even with the help of assistants, was slow, as Colin was uncomfortable with a basic text not his own. The decisive turning point came in April 1868, when Colin, on a visit to Belley, was made aware of the existence of a copy of his 1842 constitutions, which he believed were no longer extant. From that moment, he made up his mind to return to this text, which best expressed his ideas, as the basis for the constitutions awaited by the Society.

This was a potentially controversial decision. On the one hand, it enabled the work to go forward smoothly and quickly. On the other hand, it amounted to the abandonment of the mandate given him by the general chapter, which he had been trying loyally to fulfil, and the assumption—or rather resumption—of a mandate that he believed he had received from heaven. The question was: Would the Society recognise this mandate?

It soon appeared that opposition to the return to Colin's constitutions did not rest only on the fact that Favre's rule had been approved provisionally by Rome. Doubts were being placed on Colin's right to be regarded as the founder of the Society of Mary and on the originality of his rule. By now many Marists had got to know about Courveille. Was he not the real founder? What, in any case, were the origins of the original rule? Controversies over these points were not settled until 1870.

A general chapter was convoked for 5 August of that year. Favre told the assembly: 'We have met not to divide, but to unite.' They should have 'a spirit of peace and union' and avoid 'the sad example of some new societies where the general and the founder are not united and have each their own partisans'. He 'would rather die' than find himself in such a division. In order to remove the last remaining doubt, ambiguity or suspicion about where he stood regarding his own constitutions and those of Colin, he declared that 'particular circumstances' had obliged him to publish 'the rules that you know'. But now, 'the Very Reverend Father Founder gives us his work. I accept it with all my heart.'

A commission established by the chapter recognised that 'the R. Fr Colin is our sole and true founder', understanding by this term one 'who not only has thought of a work, but who organises it and gives it life'. It recommended that the chapter resolve to accept 'in principle' the constitutions presented by him. The chapter also adopted a declaration that the Blessed Virgin Mary is the real foundress of the Society that bears her name and that the members of the Society choose her as their 'first and perpetual superior'.

The significance of this declaration at the time and in its context was great: it symbolised the full reconciliation of Colin and Favre in an act in which each 'disappeared' as they and all Marists acknowledged Mary as their foundress and superior. Thus putting the origin and government of the Society on a high supernatural plane did not, of course, dispense Marists from historical investigation of the precise part played by the human instruments Mary had employed in order to establish the congregation, nor from devising appropriate forms of governance in her name. It did, however, mean that there were no further grounds to take the side of the founder or of the superior general against the other and so removed the threat of schism. It was a fine example of the 'hidden and unknown' in action.

The chapter had to be suspended, owing to the fear of revolution following the military defeat of France by Prussia and her German allies on 2 September. When it met again, in January-February 1872, it finished its work of examining and approving the text. All that remained was for the Marist constitutions to be approved by Rome. Pope Pius IX gave his assent on 28 February 1873.

On 25 March 1873, Feast of the Annunciation, the superior general announced to the whole Society the good news that 'our constitutions are definitively approved by the Holy See'. Colin considered that this act signified the end of his mission to the Society.

One more step needed to be taken. On 9 July Julien Favre convoked a special general chapter to receive and promulgate the constitutions of the Society of Mary approved by the Holy See. The chapter met on 12 August 1873. Jean-Claude Colin was there, to see the final completion of his life's work. He did not, however, take part in any of the plenaries.

Colin's departure for La Neylière on Monday 25 August took some Marists by surprise, although there had been rumours that he was about to go. But the word spread, and those members who were in the house came down, each with his copy of the constitutions. Colin entered the chapter room and dropped into an armchair. Those present asked for a last word from the founder. He managed to say a few words, until his strength gave out. He asked for help to get up from the chair. When the bystanders understood that he wanted to kneel and ask their blessing, they protested and made him stay seated. He still wanted their blessing. They began, but Colin interrupted them to ask pardon for the bad example he had given them and begged for their prayers, that the good Lord might forgive all the faults by which he had 'impeded the work of the blessed Virgin'. The chapter members insisted on having his blessing, which he gave in a rather long Latin formula that embraced the whole Society and its works, the Marists' relations and benefactors and all the members of the Third Order. They wanted to receive their copies of the constitutions from him, but he insisted that it was for the superior general to distribute the constitutions. They wanted him at least to touch and bless the volumes.

At this point, novices, other fathers and some brothers entered the room and asked for his blessing. By now his voice was scarcely audible, and he was in tears. The nearest one kissed him and everybody else wanted the same privilege. It was time to go. The carriage was waiting, and, ignoring Colin's protests, they carried him to it in his armchair. So he took leave of the chapter and Lyons, never to return.

Jean-Claude could now sing his Nunc Dimittis. But he had not yet entirely finished his work, and, though failing in strength, spent his last years working on a rule for the lay branch of the Society. This represented a return to his earlier intentions expressed in 1833.

During this time, he was cared for by Brother Jean-Marie Chognard, who, for some years now, had acted as his secretary and personal assistant and gradually became his carer and nurse. As Colin's eyesight failed, Jean-Marie wrote to his dictation and read to him, including his daily portion from the Bible—a habit that Colin had observed since seminary days. He was growing weaker; and when, in the autumn of 1875, they were beginning the Book of Job, he remarked that he did not think he would live to finish it. He died peacefully on 15 November 1875 at the age of eighty-five. His mortal remains rest at La Neylière.

The resting place of Jean-Claude Colin in the main chapel of La Neylière, since re-sited in a smaller chapel and with a new gravestone.

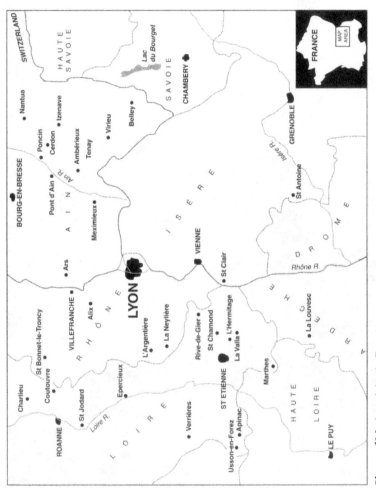

Places of Marist origins in France.